Use Words First

Edited by Jude Yawson

First Published in the United Kingdom in Paperback by:

OWN IT! and Wrecking Ball Press
Edited by Jude Yawson

Words First is a spoken word talent development scheme produced by BBC Contains Strong Language, BBC Radio 1Xtra, BBC Asian Network, BBC Arts and a variety of poetry partners from across the UK including Apples and Snakes, Neu Reekie!, New Writing North and Young Identity. This book is a celebration of the 2019 Words First artists and is a co-commission between OWN IT! and Wrecking Ball Press.

Paperback ISBN: 9781916052314

WWW.OWNIT.LONDON   wreckingballpress.com

OWN IT! Entertainment Limited Company Registration Number: 09154978

CONTENT

ABOUT *USE WORDS FIRST* AND JUDE YAWSON

Jude Yawson is the official ambassador of the Words First talent development scheme 2019, an initiative organised and run by BBC Radio 1Xtra, BBC Asian Network and BBC Contains Strong Language. It invites writers of all fashions, poets, spoken word artists, and lyricists to apply to the scheme to be a part of regional workshops and showcase their talent with the aim of developing their skills. The 12 poets who appear in this book advanced from their regional showcases to perform at Manchester Home; *Use Words First* hopes to capture their creativity on the page in a moment of time when they are at the beginning of exciting journeys as writers and poets.

Jude Yawson is a writer and published author who started writing over a decade ago, but only considered writing as a full time career at university. He writes through what he describes as 'having a necessity' insofar as he endeavours to write about underrepresented communities and create work from a wealth of possibilities that can improve the understanding between people for the betterment of society. Having graduated in BA Philosophy and studying an MA in Cultural Studies, Jude has always had a passion for creating greater representation and exploring what makes people tick to create more empathy. His writing spans across articles, essays, dialogues and film reviews and he always aims to articulate and create content in a way that is accessible and appealing for audiences who have traditionally been ignored.

Jude co-wrote and edited Stormzy's first release under the #Merky Books imprint called *Rise Up: The #Merky Story So Far*. Stormzy, who Jude has always supported and followed, appreciated the importance of representation in Jude's work and reached out to him. #Merky Books was set up for the sake of being inclusive of experiences of people from underrepresented communities, cultures and backgrounds. Jude also wrote an essay for Derek Owusu's *SAFE: On Black Men Reclaiming Space*, an anthology of work that includes a collection of essays by Black men who live in Britain writing about their experiences and multi-layered identities. Jude also regularly attends workshops and speaks at events. Jude is currently working on his own debut novel.

As the ambassador of the Words First talent development scheme, Jude attended all the regional showcases, in Edinburgh, Manchester, Newcastle, London and Bristol, watching all the performances of the artists. Jude's vision in editing *Use Words First* manifested through developing three themes: identity, connectivity, mobility and asking each poet to write two poems per theme. The aim was to encourage the poets to consider the worth of their words and their creative outlook. As a result, *Use Words First* offers an eclectic and diverse collection of poems, offering varied insights and stylistic approaches. Ultimately this is a book exploring both the self and humanity as a whole from an exciting group pf emerging poets.

INTRODUCTION FROM JUDE YAWSON

To use words first is to analyse the intricacy of what we say. We imply a lot of things; we are straightforward with most. To perform poetry is one way to deliver content. You have to think about cadence, tone, beat, as well as what's being communicated with the eyes and body to instil a vibe in a piece for the audience. It can range from solemn to comedic or sweet, triggering in one second but romantic in three.

I believe the page is another way to deliver equally emotive work, and with the words we use we play a game of communication. We incorporate so much into words, and these poets all have something captivating about them in performance that has now been translated to the page. One of the most exciting things about the Words First scheme this year is the range and depth of knowledge embedded within the poems and the way each poet has such a distinct creative approach.

The reason I chose the three themes of identity, connectivity and mobility is they are interconnected and prompt someone to think about existence as a whole. For instance, with identity I asked the poets to consider how everything they do stems from the self. I asked them what they identify with, whether that be music culture, mode of thought or orientation. Identity within the self will always speak volumes of someone's outlook, hence I wanted us all to get an insight into how these poets witness themselves through their poetry.

With connectivity I considered this internet age and the haste of wanting to be connected with each other or fear of being isolated. How connectivity plays such a huge role in existence from needing to feel connected to self, in couples, as societies or as one whole human race.

Lastly, mobility in regard to how one moves and grows: the ways we mobilise and utilise everything around us, and how mobility impacts how we see ourselves, each other and situations at different moments in time.

In exploring the themes I set out, this talented group of poets have produced a collection that unearths a variety of notions and reflections about people and life itself. In reading this I ask that you consider the poems as moments in time in these budding creatives' lives; this is what they felt and produced and shared in this day and age and it offers a great reflection of many of the ideas and themes we all think about and experiences in our own lives.

IDENTITY

HOLD A FUNERAL FOR YOUR OLD SELVES
CHRISTY KU

Everything you have ever lost is here - Joelle Taylor

Give flowers.
Dress for mourning.
Shoulder your own casket,
walk slowly.
Let the weight go.
Hold a minute of silence,
then let it all burn.
Give yourself permission to grieve.
Share anecdotes and memories,
laugh at your life.
Read old diaries like wills.
Sort old dreams like inheritances,
decide what to keep.
Ashes to ashes,
dust to stardust,
understand that
pyres birth back to a universe made of us.
Clasp your ashes
until it's coal
until you are a diamond in your own palm.
Sleep for three days
then roll back the stone.
Look in the mirror, repeat this:
'I am here now. I am enough.'

FATHER'S SON
DANNY MARTIN

On the first day of school, in a hue of excitement. He
stumbled, grazed his knee the way my pen stumbles, grazes
words on to this page. Both fabrics frayed with our over
zealousness. He is undoubtedly his father's son.

I raised him up, back to the two feet I was teaching him on
how to stand. Stabilisers are just that, your mum and I, either
side will guide your way until you have learnt to ride your
own life with two wheels.

Prior, those precious platypus feet attached to legs by rolls
of puppy fat, were held in my fathering hands. Like my
grandfather, many moons ago, I pretended that I was going
to eat them but as I approached, your toes stunk like burnt
toast. I took one whiff and withdrew. Facial expressions
gave the game away. Laughter fell out of you like Del Boy fell
through the bar in only fools. Equal measures comedic gold.
Your laugh. My heart. Your home.

Prior, sat in the Argos January sales sold spectacular
highchair, you flung food from your catapulted spoon over
everything that wasn't your mouth, Mum's designer coat
shed instant formulated tears visible on its furred skin.
Mum's disapproving words met with my undeniable grin.
'You'll be alright boy.'

You gargled your next carefully/uncarefully planned
sentences, but I knew exactly what you meant.

It was then... 'dada' followed, 'dada' your first actual word.
'Dada' – the first of infinite possibilities. 'Dada' wondered
would you grow to be a wordsmith like he was? One thing
was for sure – the world is yours to explore

'You'll be alright boy.'
Prior, Mum grasped my hand with equal measures
excitement/pain. The midwife asked if I wanted to look. I
didn't. I did. We welcomed you into the world with bursting
pride. We held your mushy head, wrinkled torso and chicken
thighs like our lives depended on it. Like our lives had just
started too. In truth, they had.
Prior, in the bed we had spent a lifetime trying to make you,
we mapped out your future from your birth to your first
word to your first day in school.
Prior, we ached in agonising unison as the doctor's words
stabbed eardrums. Echoed through bones. Sank into our
hearts. Pregnancy was no longer viable. Life no longer
possible. Miscarriage impending. The realisation of
everything that came after this moment was just figment of
imagination. Your first day at school just misguided hope.
Your platypus feet left un-stood. Your first word left unsaid.
Your father's son: if only.

EPILOGUE
RAHEELA SULEMAN

brown gurl with Simpson palms
bonsai trees instead of arms
gurl's soles keep her grounded
gurl's soul keeps her grounded
looked for the formula to fly but never found it
gurl says fuck the anti-depressant
she's been treetop-gazing since adolescence
gurl heard them yelling they want the aux cord
but she can't reach it
no one knows where to plug it in
can't find a 5-finger pin
gurl's house keys turn into a keyblade sword
she opens doors and struggles to walk in
gurl breathes out and can't seem to breathe in
gets to place and decides to leave them
gurl tries to photosynthesise for others
gurl shakes off her petals because the ground needs them
more
gurl grows a tree in the place of hope
gurl hangs her head without the rope
cuts off the right branches to cope
gurl tries to do some healing
gurl lost herself staring at the wall so she builds a cinema in
the ceiling
gurl rests in the shade still mindful of the sun's feelings
gurl never knew until now that the sunset is the sun kneeling
a greenhouse might keep her
a treehouse could keep her close

gurl could metamorphosise her woes
gurl ripped out her roots and planted herself somewhere else
gurl heard the soil is more nourishing 6ft down but isn't sure
if that's true
gurl thinks she might sleep better on the ocean bed
gurl finds her reflection in the water
calls it identity theft
splashes her distorted face
maybe she'll sway like seaweed
find a new way to breathe
tell the difference between self and other
tell the difference between sky and sea

LOST IN TRANSLATION

PRERANA KUMAR

You are the 'other' they whisper about
in Literary Theory class, voices
hitching like split matchsticks
You have campfires in your skin and
they look at you like they are
running
out of wood
You are reminded of primary school
and how you coloured countries
different
only on paper
Home says Hindi isn't spoken well
If the sounds aren't the three-kg
weights your mother bargained against
over the vegetable counter
and you are too tight-lipped since that
First plane ride
What use is a woman
who cannot scream?
Right?
Here says Hindi is not your mother
Tongue because you learned it
Second - Your mother raised you
In white dust.
You are now Tesco's measly bottled chilli powder
with salt in the mix,
You look one colour but taste another,
Not your Grandmother's hand-dried

Kashmiri chilli
Anymore
You remember how everyone ignored
her blistered hands for weeks,
but smiled as they sat down
for her creamy fish curries
How your mother slipped away quietly
to rub the aloe salve
Into her mother's swollen palms
Fit tight
in the bathroom at the back
You realise how Acceptance
Is quiet collateral paid for
In skin, how
Your mother raised you
with the language of Escape as your First,
She had it too but fell down a marriage-
carved well,
She named you Inspiration
so you could raise
Yourself
Out in her stead
And Maybe
You will always be wandering
In airport spaces by the tall windows
That box in the night-sky,
In gaps between generations and
Countries

Where Home falls into fissures
And rises as ghosts every time
They twist your name into
Syllables less
Girl, you are a violent thing,
with palms smeared Gentle
How can you wash in
Three sets of fragrance
And not come out
Like Flowers?
Maybe Home will always be the
Letterbox slit through which
Your mother sends you red fish curry recipes
the breach in your throat
Heavy corpses of Hindi syllables
sink into Gracefully,
allowing a whiter language
Refuge
Maybe Home
will be the crack in your mother's front teeth
That proudly sings of how
She pushed her daughter into a whiter
Safer Ocean
When they came howling
For her Voice

FROSTIES
LUKE AG

I used to fear starting the day
but because of you
I used to sit there with my frosted flakes and say
Today's gonna be great.
Your voice reverberates in my mind
It's like your words just rhyme
and you're not even trying
It's like you're not even speaking.
That's why your lies are so bittersweet
Because they taste so delicate,
but never complete.
I loved your quiet demeanour
The others felt meaner; they were shouting their slogans
whilst you were like me,
an inbetweener
My mama warned me about you, sugar
I used to tell her about you in the store
she told me that you'd give me pores
She'd always point at others and say
'what about them', but I was always drawn back to yours
After all,
You were the main feature of my morning routine
Whilst the adults were grinding up their coffee beans, I was
staring in your eyes
You were staring in mine
You interrupted my Tracy Beaker re-runs so readily
But when you did,
I believed that Tracy's mum really was a celebrity

I believed that Duke was a memory
and Justine was imaginary
I remember sitting there with my lunchbox on the
playground
Dreaming of you.
3.15 couldn't come around too soon
So we can be reunited together.
Pyjamas, and a bowl too big, it felt like we were watching
cartoons forever
The other kids used to talk about you too
That got me vexed
I used to hope they choked on their 'redibrek'
They thought they knew you,
but I knew you better.
You used to write to me, and I'd read every letter
I'd read every sign, between the lines
and I would mime your actions when you weren't looking
You never really spoke; you just smiled
but I used to pretend that you cared
I felt that you reconciled what I shared
and told me not to be scared.
When I was hungry for routine
I could always rely on you to be seen
We witnessed some chaotic times
but you were always there in the morning
after I was dreaming my dreams,
and you sat next to empty bottles of wine
I used to fear starting the day

But because of you
I used to sit there with my frosted flakes and say
Today's gonna be great.
I remember when I had my first beer
You were with me before my first, and next to me by my last
I remember us underage drinking in the park
You gave me the energy to take that first sip from that flask
then we lay there together on the floor,
whilst everyone laughed
I don't know why we grew apart
I think it's when I first went to Uni
and I left a lot of myself behind
My flat mates preferred avocado on toast
I preferred your crunchy design
I tried so hard to be like them
I poisoned my blood with Jack Daniels whiskey
and ate Coco Pops from a box that cost £3.50
Getting older is expensive
I guess I just wanted to be different
I wanted to change, and so did you
You changed your whole brand
You stopped being so sweet,
you started being bland
I tried to be a man and move on, tried peanut butter and jam
But the jar gave me screw faces
And the toaster had other plans
I watched you become increasingly gratified,
Spending more money on your appearance

Less time on your ambition
I remember when you interrupted me in advert breaks to tell
me your vision
But like the rest of them, you got caught up in the system
I pondered over your passions and drew patterns
with the end of my spoon
I analysed my infatuation as I wandered and waited, wanting
things to go back to how they were
Now I eat porridge in the morning
I get on the train just yawning
and enter an office with tiled flooring,
And wonder,
What you're up to now.
I sometimes talk to you, and say
'Things used to be easier mate,
Nobody's told me the truth as of late
I realise that the last person to tell me the truth was you,
when you told me,
They're going to taste great. And they did'
I used to fear starting the day
But because of you
I used to sit there with my Frosted flakes and remember what
Tony the Tiger used to
say,
Today's gonna be great.

PLEASURE
HEIDI HENDERS

I was a pleasure to have in class,
Sat in the middle and spoke when I was spoken to.
Never laughed too loud, never made myself known.
Blended in.
A pleasure to have in class.
But I bet you were the other sort,
You sat at the back and spoke all the time,
Shouted out and shouted up, to a disapproving glance and a
teacher's note.
I bet 'pleasure' wasn't the word.
And I remember boys like you.
I rolled my eyes and sighed when you spoke up.
Too scared to shout back though, 'cause your next joke could
be on me.
So, I'd just scribble the answer, and under hands I let you see.
I don't know how you came about; it's been years since those
classroom days.
I'm no longer that little girl with my shirt tucked in and A*s
in my eyes.
Pleasure means something different now.
Now maybe I didn't think with your lips against my throat.
Didn't think about what school had taught us both to be.
I just saw brown eyes and lusting hands,
And boy, the pleasure was all mine.
I've learnt different lessons now
Book smarts turned to street smarts
I learnt to love in the mirror
Dropped the knee length skirt and shy girl demeanour.

But in your hands, I suddenly felt so small
Like that quiet girl from class 1E.
You must be laughing somewhere here
An inside joke from years ago.
When you shouted out and shouted up,
And I was just a pleasure to have in class.

O' FLOWER OF SCOTLAND

COURTNEY AMA STODDART

I wish I could sing your praises
Revel in legends of ages
Hold Gaelic curled in my mother tongue
I wish I could hear her speak
Hear her song
Soft
Sweet
Unbroken
But Scotland doesn't love me like her other children
Though I was birthed from her womb
And have took shelter beneath her breast
She watched me inhale my very first breath
Her smell
Her soft tones envelop me as if I'd been here for centuries
But questioned is my lineage to her
Scotland, my mother
She shudders if I claim her as such
Looks disgusted and wonders how her bastard child grew up
so dark and brown and wild
Some seek to banish me from my mother's land
'Where are you from?'
'No but where are you really from?'
'You must like Beyoncé and know all of her songs'
'You're black aren't you?'
'What're you mixed with?'
'What are you?'
'A paki?'
'A nigger?'

Though not chased with knives like my forefathers and their
brides
I am questioned
I am ripped and torn apart
Never human yet still existing
Violence is so unremitting
In the aether I am floating
Luminiferous but still left choking
Deities rise and fall
But O' flower of Scotland do you hear my call?
While I'm dissected on this table
Cut by those that think they're able
My story told in the tallest of fables
'Can I touch your hair?'
'In fact I'm not even going to ask I'm just going touch it
anyway'
It can happen numerous times in a single day
You'll overstep my boundaries
But then again you've been doing that for centuries
I step off the bus and a group of boys call me a nigger
And trust me they knew just how to pull the trigger
Trust me they did so with vim and vigour
I walk off the bus and not knowing whether to laugh or to cry
I do both
And once again I'm in the aether
Luminiferous I hear their sniggers
But they're only half right
Cause I'm half white

And through the night I recall boyfriends
Who'd call me 'caramel princess' in front of their friends
Display me like a trophy
But never really care to know me as an entity
As a being that can laugh and sing and breathe
And then call me a black bitch when I don't do as they please
O' flower of Scotland do you hear my pleas?
Deities rise and fall
But Mother Scotland do you hear my call?
You were colonised by English men
They took your page and they took your pen
They raped your children and your women
Yet you still deny how you joined them to take more lives
And wear your flower like a crooked disguise
You lost your language
Your heritage
And I've lost mine
Eyes, mine, well with tears
See my waters were taken well beyond their years
As my ears excrete lies and untrue fears
Just a child
Rejected by the motherland
And body abused by the father's hand
Taught to sing Auld Lang Syne and let auld acquaintance be
forgot
Be one of a handful of 'coloured' kids in the school
Colouring in the sky from white to blue
In colouring books

Taken from shelves that held lies and false history
My tongue trapped beneath a heavy head
Lips too large to open
Couldn't even say my own name when spoken to
When teacher takes register
I couldn't register how to communicate
'Othered' too much
Flinch at every touch
It sealed my fate
And when placed in front of another mixed-race face
We'd both feel hatred
The reflection was too great
And still late you are to reply but I ask
O' flower of Scotland do you hear my cries?
I know it's been a while
O' how time flies
I'm sure you've been busy raining from the skies
But see my waters were taken well beyond their years
My tears never allowed to stream
My streams never allowed to trickle softly into oceans
My rivers were man-made
They were stolen and taught how to behave
My ancestry is that of slave and master
So please tell me how to move past into new pastures when
the rain of truth doesn't fall here
I see her sometimes and then she disappears
Just like me, she speaks politely
Descends in mist then rises again

It's as if we've been doing this dance for centuries
Redefining the lines and the boundaries
Luminiferous, we're in the aether
Choking, drowning, quake and quiver
And just like me, her waters were taken well beyond their
years
O' flower of Scotland
Do you hear my fears?
Deities rise and fall
But Mother Scotland do you hear my call?

ANGELS
ESTHER KOCH

I know what you think of angels.
Tender of face like nectarines.
Small as Sistine Chapel fresco babies.
Well then know that I am not an angel.
I am vicious like honey badger.
I will judge you.
I wear antique-sweet-shop-scales across my shoulders like
Libra.
I will try to change you, save you
like the lieutenant of a recovery platoon
relegated from Heaven to Earth;
real angels are cool apaths
chilled from their time wallowing
in the dregs of the atmosphere.
Angels are spies,
chameleon their skin with the midnight.
They reveal themselves only to a select few.
Light-refractive-crystal-cohorts,
Centurions with red wings, iridescent like aura-quartz
a roaring conflagration, moving imperceptibly
like tectonics, deafening
licks of fire on the Judean periphery
a molten mirage at the base of Mount Sinai
they leave glitter in the dust
while I flick blue grit from my eye like lapis lazuli,
congealed mortal silt versus
powdered, shimmering husks
through angels

God spoke to Saracens and to Canaanites
before he spoke to us with our
feet-too-good-to-foul
and our sun-dried dispositions.
We poached the devil,
we took his wings, we took and used and still use his
ivory tusks,
I'm not etched in alabaster.
I'm more plaster of Paris.
Celestial things only happen to the chaste
lions licked the wounds of Euphemia in Turkey,
miracles only happen to those desiccated by
leprosy, to the devout, to the undomesticated and to the
dirty
angels aren't born in Tooting.
And they don't know small talk.
They won't recognise curtesy because they don't exist to
please
I am certainly not an angel...
but perhaps the divine life is for me.
Flocked skin like Sylvanian Families.
Plucked harps synthesise halos and new-life and good-news
and
other fallacies.
Florescent blood in channels beneath limestone skin
grey and akin to Plasticine
fluid, shifting,
the vibrating minutiae of angels

are just chemistry
and angels are
high atomic activity
and I am love
and I am grief
and I am obsession
and I am loyalty, so I am
definitely
not
an angel?

BORDER

SAF-S2E

Brain matter by the border
Bullets by the altar
Pickled corpse in tabernacle
Piss on uncarved headstone mark where your children can't
play
The holy hallowed tips that holed a crucifix at the pulpit
72 virgins to bare the casket

Step to me I dare you
Tech nine to your dome piece
Smoked out like Reggie leaves
Ashes like dust in autumn breeze
I tattoo tallies of martyrs I birthed with bloodthirsty arousal

I'll shape my homeland hairline with broken graves

No tombstone under church made caves

I'll mark my walls so high reality barely survives inside

So be my guest cross the line
leave your body behind
Azazel awaits your arrival

This is my homeland
THIS IS MY HOMELAND!
No colonials touch base here!
Helm, Hardinge, Gordon, Kitchener

I will bathe in your blood
I will fight my wars and not yours
Justice is a product of education.

BELONG
AMINA ATIQ

I

We swerved between checkpoints, armed young men
watched from a distance, an elderly man squatting
in a dark corner, stared. A group of veiled women
on the balcony, giggled. I stuck my national flag
out of the car window – reds, whites, blacks faded.
The colour in my skin brushed against the plane
window and the wind blew me west – I was there,
in a strange land. I was there, greeted.
Soon we became friends, best friends. Too soon we
betrayed our roots, olive backcombed hair – I hated
the smell. My jet-black hair falling down my back,
too thick to carry, too different, I chopped it all off.
I was there, in glass windows and brick walls,
begging on the streets for 'Penny for a guy', watching
the fireworks display light up your new city, eat a halal
Christmas dinner, sprinkle grandma's spices – a taste
we've been trying to recreate, even if we tried.
Soon my scouse accent lingered on my tongue,
I wanted to feel wanted like that and I made sure
I did. But I slept with my mother's voice in my ear,
Never forget where you came from.
In my broken Arabic, this is all the home I need.

II

A white boy shouts from the other side, where
do you come from? I, picking at my skin, scarred
with mosquito bites to remind me what is marked

shall never be forgotten. In my perfect broken English,
I come from here.
He looks down at his hands,
Your skin is dark.
I stuck my tongue out, you wanna come out and play.
He nodded and smiled. We played Piggy in the middle
with his friends, by sunset, it was my least favourite game.
I couldn't sleep that night because there were sirens
on my TV and he looked like my uncle. Bearded, Arab,
brown eyes, olive skin. Terrorist. Terrorist. Terrorist.
It was shouted down my ear, pulling my scarf
to the ground and left me there.
I kept God in a small box and learned how to cry.

III

A white man on the bus asked me, why don't you go back
home?
And if home asked for my return,
I will return. I will meet her between
the valley and the mountains,
and you'll find me drinking water
from her palms.
But war has separated us
and I yearn to taste my mother's
bread and knock at my friend's house,
to tell her,
I do not belong here.

AN EDUCATION

TOM DENBIGH

they say if you take a new bird
in that raw eye still stuck down with albumen
state
and give it to another parent
a wolf rabbit tiger
it will believe it is that
see itself mirrored in the claws of the tiger
its cry a tiny roar
grow into the space it must be
be something it isn't
till one day you have a tiger with only the body of a bird
stalking through the grassland
not a bird
never that
just a feathered tiger
take instead of a bird, take a new-born baby
leave it in the deepest, darkest woods of all
eyes still sticky with albumen
then come back in 18 years
not to a human
but to a forest
in the shape of a man

THE MISEDUCATION OF
THE BLACK WOMAN'S BOTTOM
BIRDSPEED

MTV Base, 1996
Her bum bum is storytelling in a dialect I have not yet
learned. I want to know how to speak like that, how to make
those muscles so powerful they can scream, be heeded
across mountains. She is working it with as much spirit as
a preacher in the pit. But soon I realise no one in the music
video is praying. This is the first time I have witnessed a
black woman expressing herself in the confinements of
what is posing as Hip Hop. There are men, with gold teeth
referring to her bum as 'cake', they are gobbling it down,
spitting it back out, using her gluteus as polish for their
chains. Chains that like her butt carry the weight of Empire. I
am determined to learn anyway I know deep down she must
be saying something important.
I excavated meaning from temples and hallowed ground.
Their behinds: jittering and waving matriarchal legacies,
tipping their cores back and forth stirring a fire, saluting
passing orishas. I discovered the motherland in the rippling
of our hips and swooping of our thighs.
With a language so displaced it became a necessary ritual
for us to craft new lexicon daily; especially with the dangers
of strangers misinterpreting our conversations as 'sexy
adult talk', knowing that was but a footnote to a great
encyclopaedia of worlds and mysticism.
At sleepovers I continued my right of passage. My friends
and I studied how to: Tick - Tock mathematical equations,
Slow Whine self-love, Bubble pleasant exchanges like
'pleased to meet you sister', Dutty Whine discussions on

astrology, Butterfly about how cute Renae's neighbour was,
and we even made a wiggle for 'I was almost electrocuted
trying to conduct a scientific experiment on Barbie'.
You may call it primitive, the sassiness of our shakes
it was an ass with influence that persuaded Madagascar to
separate,
when waistlines roll it brings about good fortune
it was the laughter of African bodies that gave birth to the
moon.
Our gyrations are civilised, a fact conveniently forgotten
such is the miseducation of the Black woman's bottom.
MTV Base, 2019
There she is again, this time I am fluent in my body. She is
rocking her pelvis at a rapid pace to loosen the derogatory
slurs fastened to the arch of her back. She is aware of the
judgement placed upon her character when she behaves
like that; by convulsing her bandit muscles she is praying to
liberally speak in her strong unfiltered dialect, even if no one
else understands her. I join in solidarity, fluttering my hips
and twerking, in tongues.

AFTER ARIEL
CHRISTY KU

I played Ariel when I was 14.
every week,
post three pm rehearsals
in the big drama room,
I could take my shoes and shyness off.
we annotated scripts in pencil;
stage left, stage right,
ran the lines, repeat
ran the lines
and 'from the top once more'.
the big day:
a theatre full of schoolchildren who
actually liked Shakespeare.
backstage
we tied ribbons on our wrists
mine so tiny they trimmed the length.
onstage
you speak yourself weightless.
I don't know if I was any good
but I lost my stutter in character.
I moved light
easy
wasn't heavy inside
wanted to be alive
living
eternal
these awkward bones were graceful.
finally living like I was fourteen

no pressure, no measure
just joy.
with the help of your good hands
let your indulgence set me free.
cue applause
curtains
stepped off stage and
I gave it up.
I gave it all up.
that was the deal.
final role and
never be on stage again.
in our house you did as you were told
or you get kicked out or killed
so, for my new role
I played
obedience
play good girl nice girl repeat
play good girl nice girl repeat
when my tongue knows no impurities
I miss a whole language of defiance
I am clinging to the top of the class
below are father's fists –
a survival later.
I'm still grieving my lost storyline.
how do I go back
when you don't see people like me on a stage
not with my skin, my age.

they name me woman and
they say no
my naivety will make me edible
but I have lived through too much
I need to come back.
if they're hungry to tear young dreams apart
they can fuck off

I'll whistle and bring the lighting rig down
yell for Macbeth to come cut their necks
I'm being heard
from the royal box to the cheap seats
I'm here.
put your hands up.
give me an encore
an applause
or a surrender.

MY FRIEND SEAN 'MACCO' MCCORMACK IF HE WERE AN ANIMAL

DANNY MARTIN

Macco is a Lion, his oversized furry parker jacket hood is
his mane.
He is brave even in his impending defeat. He roars because
he has no other choice.
As he greets his tribe for one last time, oversized furry
parker jacket hood over where his hair once grew.
We see him lay on his back at the pinnacle of his cliff edged
throne before a kingdom not quite ready to say goodbye.
He bares his teeth and extends to us his paw. A show of
gracious surrender.
As if to reassure us.

That this is just the circle of life.
Our Lion. Our King.

DAY 'N' NITE
RAHEELA SULEMAN

this time the mosquito reached me in a way that ghosts can't.
this one feels defeated by the reflection,
not fully aligned with the self.
walks into the mirror and gets to the other side
yet not like the ones who foam at the mouth.
not beyond recognition.
still earthly, five fingers on both hands,
small wings,
god in the corner.
(I'm not sure if I need this next stanza)
the mosquitoes madness keeps distracting me.
I try to run but
there's so much blood
coming out now of me,
all this blood.
I caught that mosquito with my eyes closed,
heard it humming.
wiped my hand on the wall,
left the bloody print.

there's another realm out there
where I don't have to cut to see if I'm still red on the inside.
I stare into space to catch the glitch with an eye,
all I get is this mosquito bite
while I sleep through the day to
treat my grief with the night.

there's more unrest in the land of men,

but where I am no one tends to the laws,
not even insects.
It's always night when you think its day,
when a mosquito sucks your blood you can squeeze it right
back into your vessel,
when you drop something it doesn't fall,
and when you fall you float because
that's how the ghosts do it.

BIRTHSONG
PRERANA KUMAR

early baby is witch child. will not live to cry – old wives' tale

They took me from her body – sack of blood volcanoes
brimming to the top
where they tapped her
full with needles

They said she smiled shining when she heard my collapse-
lung hiccups
but the tremble set in her bones when she heard they turned
her into a living
body-pump for nothing

Heart murmur, they said
Heart murmuring till its
Tendons gave way and folded
like a collapsible
Box

They said she held me all that night and the night after as my
heart murmured till the moon rose and whispered my name
into my ears again and again
over the whispers of broiler witch-child this baby will not
live the night if she does not cry

> *(child, you will Sing songs of sarkashi for the world)*

and when Father arrived for the first time forty-eight hours

later, spade in hand, ready to measure the hole he needed to
dig in the back garden

it is a miracle!

The nurses whispered

(she'll live!)
how I still murmured in her arms and Screeched, heart full
when he took me from them and

how I belonged deeply to her the way you cannot tell between
a snake's old skin and its new scales until it has slithered
free

and how she fainted, smiling, after, in the sheets pockmarked
from leaking puncture wounds, and

how they said she refused the morphine so she could hold me,
raw belly embroidered with
thread, and

how, today, she cannot feel certain nerve-dead parts of her
body
but tells me, proudly,

I murmur when I remember what the ashes are made of

you are phoenix-born

MIRRORS
LUKE AG

For most poets, this platform is a stage, but for me
it's always been therapy
and the audience are the medics
Sometimes when I get on stage and perform
some people say 'you're sick'
Sometimes I say 'I know...
so why won't you help me?
I came here for assistance
but I only get clicks and applause
and I got so sick one time
they even gave me an award
I wonder...
If I cried on stage, would you give me an encore?'
My passions are so contorted I turned
pain into profit
Often, I'm telling the truth
but more often, it's gossip
If you think I've got integrity
then I know that I've lost it

THE FOXES ARE VOICELESS;
THE HUNT NEVER DIES

HEIDI HENDERS

The bunting is red, white and blue
The guns are pointing, outward, loaded.
The hunting begins.
You'd think the crowd would thin at the cruelty,
Truly be sickened by the shooting,
But they close in,
Their televisions tuned in,
They're all assuming these foxes have done something
wrong
Not knowing when their backs are turned their red tails give
them away.
Most of the populace is foxes these days
And the hunters they never seem to run out of prey.
But some fox keep ticking the boxes that put hunters above
hunted,
And shy away when confronted with blood-covered bunting,
And blame those foxes for getting in the way.
Say – the hunters all line up, beaming pride, glint in their
eyes, mind pinpointing the prize.
They're under the guise of being there for the people.
Evil.
Wiser foxes stand behind, shouting from the side but out of
the firing line, that's fine.
The hunters are wearing their best.
'Can't hunt well unless you do up your tie.'
They blare the national anthem
Ranting.
The hunt begins.

One goes straight for the fox cubs,
'Starve them' she screeches
They've listened to her speeches
Her demeanour inscrutable
Her shoes? Well they're beautiful.
Diamond studded.
When the foxes were bloodied she did not shed a tear.
Some foxes are quaking with fear
But still some are watching
Braying for blood
Thinking they will never be next...
On the right of the line is the people's man
Pint in hand
Swilling, spilling, and somehow he's winning.
Breeding hate for the foxes who aren't quite the same.
Gunning down and around, but wait what's that sound?
A fox rears up, turns back on the hunters.
He's grunting and gorgeous,
He's soaring, he's furious.
He draws up full height, against this far-right hunter
Who is blustering about 'boatloads' and 'protecting our
borders'
But this fox with a sly smile spits in his eye
It's frothy; it's milky
It's a moment of history
While the foxes are voiceless, the hunt never dies.
Riot ensues.
The fox in their numbers are rabid and jumping.

Spitting and kicking
The hunters give back
A big fox grabs the blonde and, in the mud, they wrestle.
Till another fox appears and twats him with Trestle.
Volumes of Marx fly through the air
And Lenin as slingshots
The hunters are there, starting to shy.
Till a fox in pig's clothing steps into the line.
He twirls his baton.
The foxes, mistaken, think he's on their side.
Till he starts to back the hunters.
The foxes they stumble,
Run. Scatter. Get underground.
The fight can't be won while they're low on their numbers.
The hunters all smirk.
Their work here is done.
The foxes still running and the pigs in pursuit.
It starts to get dangerous, not sport anymore.
The rebellion is stopped. The extinction goes on.
And the hunters all go back to where they have come from,
They swill their champagne. Roll out their red carpets for
hunters from far off who have bayonets
sharpened.
The foxes all gather, in burrows and holes
And vow to their fox cubs they'll protect all they own
The foxes are voiceless; the hunt never dies
Not while we foxes stand idly by.

IDENTIFY WITH ME
COURTNEY AMA STODDART

We walk in the shoes of slavery
and look at the chains what they've made of me
The blackness weeps yet continues to breathe
And the whiteness hides what it does not believe
Patterns weave through history as if its fate it cannot see
Lives caught in mystery cross walks through nights that
cannot sleep
Deeper still the patterns grow as if my fate I did not know
I'm dining at the table of white supremacy
A systematic dichotomy with many shades of grey
Chained at the bottom of the economy
Darwinism philosophy is inhaled as food of the gods
Ambrosia, they drink from the cup of Africa
Coltan, gold and massacres
Slavery by another name
Sickness is in lies and the remedy lies in truth
We've all been poisoned by the same damned fruit
See in the church where we learn today
The steeple is a top a spiritual affray
Adam is white
Eve is white
God is white
But go back to genesis
And they were as black as the night
White ships took flight
No end in sight to see how to put a stop to white supremacy
Strangers knock at the doors of complicity
Refusal to account for mass poverty

And philosophy and sovereignty is at stake
Freedom of thought is chained and unable to escape
They want us to intake such fakery and look at what the
chains they've made of me
The darkness cries in the highest of shrieks
And the whiteness dies atop the mountain peaks
And my speech is stuttered
Butterflies flutter in my stomach
A caterpillar locked in a cocoon
Which rose first the sun or the moon?
Can hatred transcend past the point of noon
As love befalls a certain death in waters of an ever-flowing
monsoon
It falls once
It falls twice
And with the speed of light it cuts like heart to the knife
Is life just an array of colours?
A spectrum within a spectrum?
And division underpins foundations of system
Made of people never really taught to listen
To the intricacies and the sounds
I listen to my voice I hear it now
Heads bow to that they cannot see
A system built on the backs of that which only exists
invisibly
But who's to say who's right in this life or who we should
obey
Identity

Well look at what the chains they've made of me
It seems like the antithesis of something that was made of
this
It seems we're bound by chains on wrists
As though gold chains negated this
And look at what the fates they've seen of this
A pattern weaved through history
As if it's fate it could not see

WOMEN
ESTHER KOCH

Everywhere women are eaten.
Ranchers leave their wives out to tan,
slapped on the porch like biltong
ready to chew on
then spit them out like gristle
in the dust
when it suits them.
Everywhere women are dismantled,
our bodies have margins that separate
rump from rib from loin from liver
and what is left is worn like thrift shop leather,
cut-price
bargain bucket
cheap tender
curves, like desert dunes
in the eye of an astronaut
a nut-coloured décolletage
where omnipotent hands
have kneaded skin, we are
in our element,
like wildebeest in sub-Saharan wind
and mercury, changing
because we're uncomfortable
we shift like soil;
(whereas the moon remembers
the earth forgets)
The damning tread of boots
is hidden from view.

Everywhere women are sculpted.
We are the peat that preserves the relics of men,
the mud that fortifies his home,
the grout in the mosaic beneath turquoise domes
and the balancing air between boulders
in dry stone walls,
we are the oxygen swept deep in his lungs,
entrenched in his blood,
the gas that erupts to bolster
his forearms built roman roads.
So where do all roads lead?

We're renamed.
Bed-buddy, Baby-bunker, Butter-churner,
Buttress, Protectress, Benefactress,
Composite, Requisite,
a Wreath, a Well, a Bucket Full,
a Meagre Trickle,
a Torrent, a Treat, a Staple
sieved for and salivated for like Nuggets,
and battered like Okra.
Beloved like Oprah,
everywhere women are golden.

LEGACY
SAF-S2E

See no Evil, Speak no Evil, Heed my Speak.

Think freely so long as it's what I taught you.

Give me your curiosity so long as you conclude my conclusion.

See my Facts, Speak my Mind, Hear my Lies and believe them.

Your thoughts are misspelled,

and your tears must be saltless,

Your eyes are brown as skin and you must only see my truth
with them.

See no Evil, Speak no Evil, Hear my Voice in bass.

My love is enforced through fear and I will deny the fact.

Pick my painted wisdom by blackened battle scars,

My son

Legacy is the greatest entity and my head you must hold
above the clouds.

Dreams are nothing but glorified destruction.

Your pen is a weapon and you must wield it how I wish you to,

Or your honour it will betray.

You are mine and thus your reflection will hurt mine.

See my Wisdom, Speak my Words, Do NOT Hear my Lies.

Think my mind, and my pride will shine upon thee like God
upon a prophet.

IF I AIN'T WHITE

AMINA ATIQ

You will not know of my death
je suis my name
illuminate my flag across
your skyscraper
scatter your flowers
and stand in stillness
If I ain't white.

CHECKLIST
TOM DENBIGH

I
I have imagined my own death a thousand times
in that melodramatic way
mainly by walking into the sea like my mum planned to
like my great-aunt actualised, solidified, brought into being
traditional
planned as one who knows the sea:
you'd want I think
two smooth large stones in each pocket
enough to tire you but not enough to weigh you down at first.
a shingle beach for the way shingle tends to slope steeply
down
and the ready provision of stones.
you'd want an offshore breeze
a retreating tide
and then to crawl out crawl out
at the midpoint
where the 1 2 3 3 2 1 rule applies
and the currents are strongest
you'd want it to be overcast
(if this was in despair)
but otherwise sun is fine
if it was cancer or something,
though the rays might bring people
so maybe not
you'd want alcohol
I think rum goes down best straight,
and drugs (nonspecific)

but probably codeine or similar
you'd want to swim without calculating how far back to
shore it is
how much stamina you have left
like on those long walks that go in straight lines
and are the worse for it
as your brain counts the miles back again
neck jerking round at every branch
to see the same view backwards,
no going back this time.
saved up
forgotten about
like a bookmark
not a sad thing
something for emergencies
a useful trick to use
if needed
but always the worry
always
that a child will find the limp body
after I have finished with it

II
come to Devon
not for what the posters say
not very Enid Blyton,
come for the sea and sand
come for the ice cream, more cream than any other

stay for the option of death
just forty metres offshore

ROSE GOLD
BIRDSPEED

I am my close friends
my cool fascination with
quantum physics and
pattern mixing in day wear.
It took time to define me.

Now a suitor calls
asks that I crumple my clothes
wrinkle time and space
to make way for a love life,
to share an identity.

As girls we daydream
have planned so many weddings
with no groom in sight.
I never considered I
would have to share so much me.

Definition years
sold at the whimsical slip
of a rose gold ring.
Let's go on an adventure,
travel back to when we grew

CONNECTIVITY

TRIPPING UP ON HEAVEN'S DOOR
CHRISTY KU

while I yet live let me do dumb shit still - Gboyega Odubanjo

I have mistaken strangers for brethren
and had to small talk my way out.
Pocket dialled the same person six times,
cried upon wearing the wrong shoes to school,
left lip-balmed kisses in Christmas cards for crushes,
dawdled and daydreamed into a ghost of myself
lost my voice in the presence of mortal angels
slurred and mixed up my words until
my tongue was the Tower of Babel
and men scattered
and I spoke a language of myself.
And yet may I live
so at the gates of Heaven,
reading my book of deeds,
God Himself is laughing.

LONDON'S DISPOSABLE CAMERA
DANNY MARTIN

Night buses. Liquid lunches. 2-4-1ers. Bottomless brunches.
Cheap dinners with credit crunchers. One-night lovers.
Friday night beauties. Saturday morning munters. I love
this city. No stopping. 9am clock in. 8 hours daydreaming.
Weekend drinking. Evening beer gardens. 'You've had too
much mate.' I beg your pardon? Stick another one in there
for the road: Carling. Bouncers starting. Swiftly departing.
Next morning café debriefs with the boys as standard.
Laughing. White lies. White lines. Double yellows. Parking
fines. Red route. Red light. Bun zoots. All rise. High rise
flats. Flat packed furniture. Flat out yawning on a Sunday
morning rushing to remain a church servicer. Blessings.
Confessions. Confessions of a call girl. Small world but two
worlds. Austerity. Don't know who lives next to me as we
don't talk to our neighbours. Exchange sexual favours for
ungrammared but complimentary texts. Tinder, swipe right,
who's next? Pound of flesh. Sexual health checks. Maybe it's
us that's fucking the NHS. Cuts to all government spends.
We do have Boris bikes though... so we wheelie down the
Hampstead road with our middle fingers up through no bike
zones. Make yourself happy at all costs. Laundry baskets
filled with crusty socks. 5k runs. Dust off, the weekend sesh.
What even is fine dining at the Ritz without an Eton mess?
Boat race. Rat race. Paper chase. Train delays. No morals in
a pound note. Rolled notes. Everyone has a friend named
Charlie. Vegan sausages on the barbie. House party 'cos
the pubs are all gastro. Fiddle expenses to aid cash flow.
London's Fidel Castro. Communism. Capitalism. Capitalise

on moral indecisions. Undecided. Divided political stances all come together for Notting Hill Carnival dances. Dance off with feds. Criminality carried out on peds. Play Simon Says with our silenced stress. P-E-D's prescribed at gyms. Instagram every fucking thing. That's how we eat in 2019. Take 9 e's at every festival 'cos we overdose on car fumes and overwork on same pay overtime, so you best believe we also overdose on sunshine and good vibes. I love this city.

THE PIXAR LAMP FORGOT HOW TO JUMP
RAHEELA SULEMAN

I don't want to die as much as I want to control,
as much as I want to control buzz lightyear and breathe life
into him.
as much as I want to Ctrl+A and drag and drop myself in mid-
air.
I'll ask the paperclip to walk me through the apocalypse,
force to quit,
I might even fuck up this whole computer.
infiltrate the entire system,
program a digital coup,
emerge into a moth and sit on a screen in the dark.
I'll shout WORLDSTAR at the top of my lungs,
bid my vital organs on eBay,
log the date of my death in a google doc and give just
anything breathing permission to edit.
I want to empty the recycling bin while I'm still in it,
mute the YouTube video to lip read instead.
play sims 2 in my room and befriend the grim reaper,
cheat death and lose a couple lives,
watch a GTA sunset because I fear to look outside.
I don't want to die as much as I want to control.
as much as I want to be the invincible empath,
the waterproof phone case,
as much as I want to chuck this glass of juice on my keyboard
smash my head against the monitor until I see blood.
I want to livestream my view from the grave
show up as 'dead dude' on the caller ID.
I want to walk into my room and watch buzz lightyear keep

doing his thing out in the open.
if I can't be the manipulator, I could be the cousin to that,
player one.
convincing us of inanimate living,
real actualisation,
incarnation,
immersion.

A LETTER TO READ WHEN THE PLANE LEAVES
PRERANA KUMAR

Mama,
Look, how we break within the hour like rain.
Like how curry with too much malai splits early

Look, how we have always clung to the least of each other,
wrapped around
our little fingers, a tapestry of old thread
sewn between us

I stole your gold earrings when I was five. I did. I did not
say earlier because you have the woman habit of gathering
others' shame and sewing
it into your wrists

I forgive you for when we danced – You, with my hair
streaking your palms, like old cobweb henna,
You, weaving them rough out of my scalp making footwork
markers on the floor

I stole your earrings, but you cannot touch me for lying, you
did it every night telling Him how I had been a good girl
who gave no problems none no, no

Come, I will buy you some cloth for your trouble to pattern
like grandma patterned you
like you would've done me if I hadn't left

I know you've hidden my scalp-strands in your mirror box

where the earrings once lived
A last reminder of the one dearest thing
you loved and hated enough to let go

This is how we tally sin, you sewing away, late into the night,
the least of me wrapped around your wrists

The thread runs out long before
I get to the basket

THIS CITY
LUKE AG

This city has its own vocabulary
Where the root meaning of failure is to succeed
and ambition is nothing but a synonym for greed
I'm not sure if you agree, but the language of this city isn't
written in words
It's in the way that you talk and the way that you're heard
Seen in the way you walk, and judged in the way you've
learned
The language of this city is written like a melody
with the saddest of lyrics, look
We sing the chorus together, like an exoteric book
But, the rest of the verse is easily forgotten
The chorus is the only thing we have in common.
But you can find interpretations
Graffitied in the tunnels of Waterloo station
The Saturday night sounds of Shoreditch offer a narration
But, the language of this place is changing...
This space we live in has increasingly less choice,
So, I write poetry because the only thing I can use for free, is
my voice
... and I still have to pay for you to hear me
Living in a world where conversation's not free
Because I gotta pay £40 a month to stay on my 4G
This city listens, in the same way as those grey ticks turn
blue
and my mind races, as I think, whilst this city,
This city thinks of words, as I do too
So why can't our city reply?

ZARA
HEIDI HENDERS

It's 9pm and Zara is measuring her worth in Instagrams
Locked in a drama with Taylor Swift fans
Over a typed-out comment about her favourite band.
What started as banter, soon descends to disaster
'Cause Zara is 14 and this is all that matters.
Her reputation is in tatters, her fan-page fan base rapidly
declining,
As the tween terror trolls are mining every picture she's ever
sent.
Every selfie she's posted.
Once 10k followers she boasted,
Now falling by the thousands.
These kids in glass houses are throwing stones at their
screens,
Mean and obscene in their insults.
And Zara is crying alone in her room.

She's having every one of her flaws pointed out online
By strangers who can't see how she cries
Tied into this 2D 4-inch-wide plastic world.
She's clutching her phone in her fingers,
Till the grooves of the buttons are embedded in her skin.
And though the metal is thin it starts to feel heavy,
Messy, melting, molten,
She drops it.
The argument started at 4,
And since then she's sat connected.
Phone plugged into the wall,

All her energy fixed on the blue light glow.
'No' was the answer when her mum offered her food,
Her parents are used to her being rude,
They just think their 14-year-old girl is in a 14-year-old's
mood.

Zara glances around at her now dark room.
She thinks it must be bedtime soon.
She presses her phone to check the time but the numbers
slide out of view.
She blinks, tries to right her vision,
The room starts spinning.
She feels nauseous, too cautious to move,
The world-wide weight of the web is wrapped around her,
Drags her downward,
And despite the thousands of friends at the ends of her
fingertips
Spread across the globe, ether-string connections
All she feels is alone.

She gets to her feet,
Her phone still buzzing on her bedsheets,
And breathes.

She can hear her parents talking in the kitchen,
Pulled by the voices, real and rich and rising,
She leaves her phone behind her.

THE OTHER
COURTNEY AMA STODDART

So, you found a new group
They're white and they accept you
Well – they don't reject you
They may as well fucking elect you
Cause now you're transgressive
And they sure as hell are progressive
But the message
In media and culture remains the same
It's engrained in the brain and it won't be explained but it
will be sustained
Through systems of oppression so now you're alone with
depression
And never question, the imperialist system
And its white individualism and all the other isms and
schisms
That keep you locked in the prison of colour
Caste they say – it's a blast from the past
But it remains affected and you remain rejected
And now a mixed-race man has been elected
So surely now problems of race are antiquated
After Martin Luther King, racism's just dissipated
It's eRACEed, it's misplaced and it's about anything but race
Yet some of us have to go back to black everyday
Imprisoned by colour and the systematic depiction of the
'other'
And when you do protest, you're told in laughing jest
That you are projecting false trajectories of race
And now you're the one that is perpetuating inequalities of

etymology
With no basis in biology or actuality or fact
Well I refuse to step black
I stand black and white
I stand in and out of colour
It's politicised and contextualised historically
And the narrative is written and interlaced with disgrace
No wonder you can't find your place
Cause you to have literally been eRACEd out of history
You have no authentic narratives so you can't even be
comparative
You don't exist
And offensive is your very presence
And yet too your acquiescence and acceptance of the system
that you've been put in
Is making you a participant in the imperialist ideology that
has no foundation in philosophy
Or in peace and democracy, this illusion of 'meritocracy'
So, conform, conform
Cause you'll never fit the norm
Which means your performance of the self will always be
judged by media representation
And until we can gain a re-education to then change the
inter-racial relations
You'll remain displaced, 'mixed race'
With distaste and shame
Even with a British name
You're still way out the game

You won't be selected for the team and don't even dream of
trying to play by the rules
Cause even if you use the tools provided by the state
In the institutionalised eyes you remain a 'state'
With a black-tainted fate
A problem
And again, not the norm
So, conform, conform
And if you look at what media represents black to be
It's key for seeing the dehumanisation of a collective of
peoples
Never seen or treated as equals
I stand black and white
I am dark and light
I stand in and out of colour
Refuse to be seen or treated as 'the other'
I am a human being
Can you not see I'm fucking breathing?

KEEPING POSTED

ESTHER KOCH

and Sophia Bush posted a link
because she couldn't be arsed writing anything herself
and Jamie Lee Curtis posted
'AssaultWeaponsBan'
15 times
is also the number of Halloween films she will eventually
appear in
hard-hitting stuff
and Leonardo said
something about bottle caps
before he took another 21-year-old to bed
later that day Captain America shared his disgust
at such senseless killing
but only after having MAGA emblazoned on his shield
which he then threw
at 2 dozen men
Reese Witherspoon is calling her congressman again
exactly what I would have done
in fact, I have our mayor's personal number right here
beside Nicole Kidman's and Jeremy Corbyn's
he will surely stop all those guns
and Liam Neeson said nothing
because he wants to kill the black bastards
and Russell Crowe said nothing
for fear the N word might slip out
it was suggested in the White House
that changes might be made
the priority being

Melania's name
maybe Blanche or Bianca
not Blanca of course but perhaps
Jane Jessica
Jacqueline has a good rep
and has been available
Diana would be swell
between Ross and Spencer
it's certainly more inclusive
much better
as it's discriminative really isn't it
to put the word 'melanin'
on such a pedestal
not right either that Kanye should call his kids
North but not South
Saint but not Sinner
and then there was a lot of
all black people are criminals
and all Mexicans are rapists
and all people struggling with their mental health are gun-
wielding murderers
and so, I think to myself
'Is this what it feels like to be oppressed?
Is this the experience of the minority?'
No
of course it's fucking not
because I'm white and I went to school and I have access to
free healthcare and I live in a more

economically developed country and I'm not subject to
unfair-trade and I've never worked a 12-hour
shift in my life let alone 23 hours and I have the privilege of
travelling the world with the fortified
status of a British national
and I skipped the queue on my flight from India because they
thought I was Twiggy
and people have said I look like Twiggy
and I wish I looked like Twiggy
so I think I know what it feels like
to want for much
and I can call myself an empath
because I read an article in the Guardian and it made me cry
and my CV reads that I am a people person even though I can
only tell my sister that I love her
over SMS
and I have a £500 phone but I can't bear to receive a phone
call
and I know that I'm woke
because I know
that you can't say Third World anymore
it's not about the winning you see
not about who's first
it's about the taking part
said the unmanned aircraft to the populous Near Eastern
town
said the boy-gamer cached in his room
building his own semi-automatic

when he shot the congregation, who didn't realise
that they were the Deontay Wilder to his Tyson Fury
and what I mean by that is
there is no fucking winner
violence isn't a contest
whether it's now or next year
you're still gonna get KO'd and
someone will fight dirty and
people will keep dying but we won't change the channel
and the rules will be broken
and chaos will ensue
so we'll stick to saying stuff in 280 characters
to make us feel secure
one cheat day a week
I'll stimulate my glutes now
and my heart later
I'll take my fiancé's name
and if it's Anglican that's double money
I've only got so many words so I'll announce the date now
and my condolences to El Paso later
that is if you didn't stop reading this
360 characters ago
I'll keep you posted.

MOONPIE

SAF-S2E

Mama told me I was great
My mother told me I was evil
I stole
her heart
was never mine
But I wanted it
I thought I needed it
6 years pass and moonlight is still something I wish I could
hold.
My father's sister told me I'm my father without the rage
But she didn't realise I smoke to keep cool a 4,4 barrel
And her daughter said the one I marry should count her
lucky stars
But diamonds will not place on a finger
Conscious coitus is a waste of time.

I'm not worthy of a second life
My uncle told me a man is made by a wife
A rapper told me a man is made god by his way of life
My holiday with Lucy told me I was half man, part deity.
Self-worship is sinful, but narcissism is necessary.
I think I know why the dog howls at the moon
And moon light is recycled sunlight so why do I not long to
hold the original?
Mama said she'd miss me, I haven't seen her since 13,
My mother said she loved me, but I can't remember the last
time I hugged her
That's my count

I called
her
mind was never mine to probe
But I wanted to,
My heart told me I needed to
I haven't seen my moon light in 40 months now
There's a diamond on her left hand now.

THE WEDDING

AMINA ATIQ

Inspired by 'Kayo Chingonyi', poem Kung'ana from the
collection Kumunkanda.

An English newsreader told me
home was a lost young man
holding his AK47 with no shoes:
a story that didn't tally
with my mother's childhood
memories, dancing two step
Baladi across the yard to the music
her tongue crafts. She flutters
her Turkish silk headscarf across
her shoulders.
Veiled women watch from the Balcony
and the village men gather, honking
their Toyota jeeps, firing their gun shots
to the two step Baladi across the yard.
Father wears a white silk robe
and a red and white shawl, swinging
his Janbiya to the committed clapping.
Gran-ma's blissful tears promise
mother that this is a blessing
from God.

FOR QUEER EYES ONLY
TOM DENBIGH

I wanted to write a poem for you
for me as well
for those past selves and future ones,
in honour of that moment of bone-deep exhale
when you realise the girl opposite you at work is a lesbian
(thank god there's someone in this office who is)
and you can have a quiet conversation about it in the kitchen
when no one else is there
I wrote your poem in coloured handkerchiefs
stuffed in the back of all my jeans
and hung it on the washing line to practice
singing in the breeze.
I snuck it into the pockets of strangers
(yellow – water sports)
who marched it down the road
spread your poem
(red – fisting)
with every spread leg
colour bursting out of denim
joyfully orange (– anything goes)
but then there was a BuzzFeed article about hanky codes
so, it wasn't just for us anymore
I transcribed this poem
into drag queen memes
making my message a contact sport
spelled out with drink sips and raised eyebrows
from seasons 1–3
but then Jimmy Fallon

and well-deserved popularity
killed that one
didn't they
but it's not like they didn't steal most of their language
from ballroom
anyway
aw Jesus, gross
so, I fucked the words
into the soil
at Clapham, Hampstead and Hyde
spelt it out with penis pointillism,
but the smell of semen was drowned in dog shit
and the holes were used for mini golf
I pinned this message to a toilet wall
studded it onto leather harnesses and arseless chaps
and rolled it into one of Marlene Dietrich's cigarettes
so, she could blow it out
in languid puffs
I just wanted to give you something that was ours
to hold
to hold you back
but on the way here
I dropped my notebook
and the guy that picked it up
pulled the ink away with his fingerprints
I don't think it's stealing
it's curiosity
it's care

it's boredom with your own
it's the shine
the glamour
the
draaama
of it all
but I do think it's stealing
sometimes
when there's no space at Pride
in gay clubs
in conversation
so I want to give you this
just for you
when you take away the sex
there is a still a
delight
to it all

BLACK WOMAN'S GIF
BIRDSPEED

Exaggerate my likeness with your thumbs,
smear the syrup over Aunt Jemima's pancakes,
fluffy and fat like a mammy,
squeeze her for taking care of you,
assisting your exclamations and witty remarks,
bulging lips, finger snaps, dramatic eyes
snatching her wig in a loop,
delivering life to your social media feeds.
Scroll and select your Black character for today,
download her antics and become massa,
you tell me 'it's only a little fun',
you tell me 'it's free'.

I DIDN'T KNOW I WAS LYING WHEN
I SAID WE'D ALWAYS BE FRIENDS
CHRISTY KU

somewhere, we're still 16
on a coach back to a place we both called home.
you're sleeping against my shoulder,
your jacket bundled as a pillow.
we can only see the next strip of road
lit by headlights as we hurtle
through red and white pinpricks.
inside, the dimmed light
fights the encroaching dark.

SPOTS
DANNY MARTIN

I
I was really spotty as a teenager, so for those seven years I
felt an utter failure, book smarts don't
seem to count when you're ugly.

II
I often think back to if then was now and how would I have
fared, in a playground where it's not just
insults – it's cyber warfare.

Would my mum still tell me not to worry, and that life at that
age is just make pretend or would I have
to tell my mum that unfortunately, it's not just 9 – 3.
Facebook doesn't stop at the weekends.

How do kids ever grow to be mentally healthy? When all
their lives are measured by is how many
likes they can get on their selfies.

When I grew up there was google search safe filters, kids
grow up now to Instagram – Valencia
Clarendon face filters and hate filters into the comments
behind their keyboard warrior Twitter fingers.

When I grew up it was a hate-filled cycle, full of hate-filled
teenagers riding one hate-filled handed
upon their chopper bicycles.

2019 and it's still a hate-filled cycle, full of hate-filled
teenagers, just now writing one hate-filled
comment on pictures of their decided rivals.

Would I have been one of those? Who knows but kids do
anything to fit in so I could have turned into the biggest troll.
When I grew up trolls were green haired; placed on top of
our pencils and lived under bridges, trolls
nowadays are grey floated head Twitter default pictures that
make kids throw themselves off bridges.

When I grew up, I could go home shut the door block out the
world and that was great, kids now can't
even escape notifications in their pockets from their 'mates'
and if you want some proof just check out
the suicide rates since 2008. Which coincides with the rise
of social media start dates.

They aren't going to die but our kids might if we don't teach
them in schools and at home about being
safe and kind online.

I was really spotty as a teenager so for 7 years I felt an utter
failure, but I think back to if then was now
and how I would have fared and to be fair I'm not quite sure
that I'd still be here.

So be kind.

VERSION 2.O

RAHEELA SULEMAN

these mirrors in the dark are barely sufficient.
the same goes for internet connections
and sometimes; they lag
so I sit on the home page
call over my friend
smash the screens.
watching them from the length of a hypnotist's arm.

I am clinging onto the hours,
I asked the clock hands for directions.
looking into a face and an analogue are the same,
I am trying to see colours that do not exist
because I lost my senses in the blues.

camo blue,
map of blue,
blue for my unaccounted dreams,
cobalt blue,
background characters in a Simpsons' episode blue,
I took the blue pill because I know my truth,
I have only talked to a blue screen today.

my human dimensions are never intact.
robotic limbs are scarce,
the pixels never resurrected
and a lot of us are in need of software updates.

I'll lean on walls,

how the kids on corners do.
I'm just glad that they have somewhere to meet.
a place to cross their borders without straying too far from
the signal.

THREE NIGHTS
PRERANA KUMAR

Streetlight in soft swirl bursts. Cocooned edges, only curves.
First night, you cannot believe a light so soft. He has crooked
teeth, a language your heart cries years in, silver, nestled
in the gaps. There are ripe words you pick from the dying
orchard of your heart, held out in shaking palms. His mother
tongue settles on the edge of your mouth. Believe again, in
the strength of prayer song.
He does not owe you anything. He lets words slip like
running water and you catch them; soft swift fish under your
tongue. Hold them with the thirsty belief of a valley, your
throat thick tight shut with the effort. Not his fault that you
do not spit. Second night, you shake so much, bangles ring in
high chimes. Your body, already afraid of this. How you curl
gently into him. The violence of it.
There is a curse in your blood that foretells this; how you
always drop into petals and traps and arms of men who
can bear to hold you for only three nights. Last night, red.
Fringe tissue splits somewhere, the inside of your elbow. You
run bare-legged, wet with new rain to his voice. You wait
to watch him turn in his sleep, eyelashes fluttering against
warm blush. Then settle. You are silent as you leave for the
last time, your language in his mouth, animal with grief.
At the crossroads home, you rupture, brilliant sunset, No
sound, all the blood.

UNLIKELY PLACES
LUKE AG

Cities of dreamers, healers,
Tough demeanours and passionate teachers
Cleaners, leaders, all beautiful creatures
Caught up a melody so seamless
From the flawless to the cautious
I see people with bigger dreams and smaller portions
Where smaller screens cause bigger distortions
I find myself often reformatting a page
making decisions without acting my age
Phone screens refracting the page
whilst the stress of the city stops me from adapting to
change.
We're all trying to make ends meet through digital means
But ends don't meet, and we dream
through digital screens.
But this city's always changing... A city of spaces,
cultures, races,
people from all different places
A mosaic of people with determined faces.
Wake up and look outside, you haven't done that in ages
Look at the people around you, your community's ageless
So grow old, grow gracious
But you're never too young to make changes.
Be courageous
Because change starts in the most unlikely of places.

LITTLE SNIPPETS OF LOVE POEMS (OR A FEAR OF COMMITMENT)

HEIDI HENDERS

There is a dirty rain tapping on the window, but it is sealed tight and we don't let it in.
The two-inch mile long gap in between us is gaping, and I'm waiting for you to cross it.
*
You are ever constant on my mind.
I am in a hotel room alone, thinking aloud.
*
You are a substance; you are underneath my fingerprints.
I am scraping.
*
The sky grows dark around us and I find that I don't mind.
I don't watch the time or want to say goodbye.
*
You are dirty air.
Coating each breath from my lungs, but I refuse to cough you up when you are not meant to be there anyway.
I refuse to cough you up to hurt myself, when you are intent on clinging.
*
I scrub away slithers of you in the shower, but you creep into my bed, thoughts of comfort and closeness and I recoil from the covers.
*
I am cold,
And you—
You are fire.
You are hot coals.
You are burning.
And I—
I am cold.
*
You are unrequited.
I'm undecided about what to think about it all.
*

You are summer nights, warm breeze, ice clinking, fire sparks.
You hand me a drink, I take the glass but take no sip.
*
I am not connected.
In fact, I'm feeling far.
*
You are cavernous,
And I am lost.
Not sure how to reach you,
Or if I want to yet.
*
I am happy,
You are happier.
*
I'd like to smile like that someday soon.

500 YEARS
COURTNEY AMA STODDART

Society run on confliction
Addiction and infliction of pain
Again and again just the same old stories and the same old lies
They stole us, stole our gold and ignored our freedom cries
Africa – Golden land our life was in our hands
An educated nation
That paved the way for civilisations for years yet to come
Yet from the bases we run,
Motherland tore apart, children everyday getting shot in the
heart
But click start, it's the tv again just the same old stories again
and again
Stories of fame, celebrities, parasitic royalty and illusions of
free democracy
Don't give a shit that people are dying
As long as we don't have to hear them screaming and crying
Happy to bow down to politicians murdering and lying
Too busy drinking, gossiping and buying
Lost in our worlds of sex and body image
Meanwhile politicians and priests are molesting kids,
And that filters down so it's happening next door
But why the fuck would you care unless the kids were yours?
Do you care that the shirts on your back are made by child
slaves?
But we disregard it because they have dark faces
Well quite clearly, we're not educated on races
Cause if so then we would know the caste system is there to
put humans into their places

White at the top and darkest at the bottom
And the darker they are the more likely we are to bomb them
Enslave them, kill and rape them
We should be shamefaced with disgrace that just because of race
We displace and negate heinous crimes
With neither reason nor rhyme
People on the other side of the world – whole nations torn apart the deaths of boys and girls
Genocides in disguise
So many millions have lost lives, but we don't give a shit we just buy buy buy buy
And the truth is that I am to blame
I listen to the same old stories again and again
So conditioned by my very existence
I have seen the resistance but I'm afraid of losing smoking and drinking
And capitalist thinking
And telling the same old stories again and again
As if we can't explain how our privilege occurred
Our privilege is a curse, even worse than that it is a disease
Back pages of newspapers dedicated to refugees drowning at sea

But this war that they are fleeing from was caused by
Britain's bombs
Weapons the US sells and produces
And we carry on making excuses not to take action focus on
too many distractions
Programmed and superficial interaction
Free ourselves from enslaved state full of narcissistic
character traits
Water is harder to acquire than Wi-Fi yet still we bow to the
hierarchy sky high
500 years of slavery
How much longer are we going to let it be?

DAUGHTER
ESTHER KOCH

Mothers walk their little witchlets
round and round the garden like a teddy bear,
Mothers in Waitrose hear a babe scream
and collectively chant
someone's tired
because in the night-time restless children become one
polymothered-child.
Easier then, for mothers to
exorcise the vicinity
of Banshee and Jack Lantern,
poltergeist and evil-eye,
Chupacabra and Chimera,
devils and duppy, kappa and lamia,
mothers' station an infantry
of foo dogs at the foot of baby's crib,
mothers have magic breastbones that soothe colic,
mothers carry shanks,
not shanks of lamb because youth is sacred but
beef shanks, pork shanks,
steel shanks sharpened on millstones
ready to plunge into bogeymen,
mothers have no time for
Good Friday, Lent, Halal, Kosher, Conscience, Altruism,
Common Decency, veganism or
pescatarianism,
they are conditioned to unconditionally
kill and feed kill, and feed kill and feed,
mothers are heathens,

mad mad mothers stampede
through superstores and glass ceilings,
mothers go to food banks in their electronic tags,
mothers aren't proud, they reserve feelings,
mothers work work work work work
when you gonna learn learn learn learn learn learn
that their kids take their heart and their keys and their
patience,
mothers are fluorescent stars from the planetarium
still on your wall by your 20th Jubilee
and then mothers are a fly on that wall
until your wife finds a way to extricate mum's key
to your flat,
mothers talk to one another,
mothers are an affliction of knowledge
so frightening:
the bigger and furrier the feet
the more flawless the birth,
the boy born from
uterus like a conch shell
that twists and turns
will be a hermit,
if you rest your phone on lacklustre belly
whilst watching EastEnders
unborn becomes part of the circuit.
Little baby-battery.
And as you do your chores
mum-to-be

be sure to walk in
fallopian shape, ovary to ovary
around the house
so baby knows her way out
and when you are out of her baby, make no mistake,
you are still in her keep
and she will weep a moat around you
and scrawl the magic word to your release
in her knickers
where inhospitable conditions
make her unfit for public consumption
and disqualify her from recourse to public funds
this is the lot of mums, I digress;
Female erogenous zones must first be untenanted by
dependent offspring, must re-assimilate
accordingly to the norms of post-constructed-reality and
must contribute tax by way of money
invested in menstruation, menopause, psychological and
gynaecological support, hair, beauty
and childcare.
mothers make an entrance,
walk in walk out to a fanfare
grow, cut and collect their hair
and send it 6000 miles away
for another mother to wear.
When the time comes
when mum's back
feels like flour packed tight in a hemp sack

and you realise that more than anything
you long to burrow your way back into her body
like a pantry bug,
you'd let her swipe at you again
and send you to bed,
look deep at you and make you
Fabergé-egg-eyed again
because only what creates you breaks you,
she's a crucible of molten glass and she blew you into this
fragile thing,
mum knew you before
the tough and the testosterone,
the ego and the inhibition,
a bulb never shattered in the hands of Edison
mum you are my engineer,
a lifelong subscription
and then a gold frame
in the hall, by a candle,
that you nudge so that her eyes fall
on your comings and goings so that you think twice,
once for yourself and once for her
when you fasten the safety latch
and carry your key in your fist
late at night

DARK VELVET AT FULL MOON
SAF-S2E

They brought their cherry red human transporter to a stop,
The velvet haired one turned and pulled the dark one in for a hug,
The hug lasted unusually long,
They held like sloths on a tree,
The velvet haired smiled and enquired on a possible remit.

That's when tension held like soft stone,

The dark one blasphemed by denying reacquaintance
With the confidence of a demoted demi-god he vowed to be a ghost,
At least in the eyes of the velvet haired's moonlit spirit

And that's when she questioned his loyalty,
She questioned his manhood, his ego and the fabrics of the dark one's existence.

Her olive skin was beyond his reach
They spoke of friendship
He spoke of eternity
She spoke of eschatology in relationships through code
He gave hope to promotion in code
They called each other homio
She said she'd miss him
He said he would miss her too, that's why he had to leave.

The dark one was too dark inside to rise in rank.

His lips were too black from kissing stinging cherries
Her's was pink from existing.

They spoke their goodbyes through their eyes
And held each other for the last time.
Saltwater floated down her sun kissed cheeks and dripped
onto her velvet hair.
His dark figure stepped out the red transporter and closed
the door behind him.

She drove

But just before she turned to disappear, she screamed, 'I'll
see you in June'
Then in reply he whispered, 'nah I'll see you in three
lifetimes'.

RAINBOW
AMINA ATIQ

His mother had never seen a rainbow
stretch it's wings across a battlefield
that peels its own skin and cries
for comfort she seals its mouth and waits for a storm
to swallow its pain that breathes in the cracks
of the streets where bones cradle each other
like a baby in her arms
shaking to the song of a lullaby echoing the voices of what
once
was a heartbeat of a son that clenched
its lips on her nipple until he moved his
cheek and stretched his small legs
into a man who chose love in war.
His mother crouches on the doorstep
where he had skipped and sang his
favourite song like a melody that stabbed
her through the air.
His mother waits for his return she counts
the days–weeks–years but her blistered hands
and her weary eyes fall in despair.
Until one day, he came home wrapped in a white
cloth with his eyes sealed and his puffy face.
His mother clenches in her arms like a baby
shivering to death.
What is life when memories are made
of ghosts and a rainbow that vanishes
before she could look up

PPM

TOM DENBIGH

the fact is they're not
facts until they happen
that terrifying tearing sound
as future is ripped into single present.
as graphs jaggedly jump settle twist
but always moving out of the dotted theoretical into
the thick red line
of past
fact
did you know statistics are often a couple of years old?
the emissions data is present
but papers take so long to get published
or data to be reviewed
that the panic
is last year's
or the year before's
really
the graph will show us choking
long after it has already happened
do you know at 1000 ppm our brains will shrink by twenty
per cent?
and that this could happen by 2100?
children born today
destined for tiny brains
and rooms for the rich to live in with lowered CO_2
What's there to write about
nothing more than this.
all the things the world could become

shrink by the day
with each jerk upwards of a thick red line
Jesus fucking Christ
it's too big to write about
too boring
too slow
too fast
these gasping moments of realisation
slowly sink into our existence
like waves
like day to night
like a CO_2/Time graph with
winter/summer
dip/surge
shooting upwards
into infinity
with gentle undulations

eTRAGEDY
BIRDSPEED

How can I trust the outcome of data from loneliness and
desperation?
A picture taken on the good side,
filtered and well lit
hiding, every flaw like discontinuing eye-contact,
darting into the chest of a waitress pouring another man a
drink.
Now, you want another woman,
and you want to be another man,
the kind who can afford a premium online service,
where the formalities are not necessary.
Harmony:
Where the people are real
and the creases in faces deepen,
we catch each other's eyes
during our first encounter,
toss the net into the air
trusting they will return.
How can I trust a computer to tell me if you exist?

MOBILITY

HAUNTINGS
CHRISTY KU

before boarding up a skeleton house
before skittering footprints on the gravel path
before you brought the bones in every garden you walked in
before all the teeth you buried start talking amongst
themselves
before crawling down the stairs choking on smoke
before your body hitting the floor
before the knife went in
before you said who's there who's there who's there in the
mirror
and your own reflection appeared holding the knife
before the writing on the wall spelled out your name
before you turned on the lamplight and nothing was there
before you felt cold and unalone
before you dreamt of every house you have lived in and left
before lying in a new unmade bed
before boxes and contracts stacked like golems
before the moving van broke plates like poltergeists
before your life got so heavy you needed a moving van
before red marks as crates tried to cut fingers to the bone
before bubble wrapping your breakables
before you folded yourself into neat piles
before you hugged pot plants, carrying small earths against
your chest
before you tried marie kondo, touched everything, found joy
in nothing, packed it anyway
before buying more furniture to make less space for demons
before decorating, and redecorating

before taking out the carpet with the stain
before you died the first time and your ghost packed your
bags
before you stopped being happy.
before, you felt at home.

A WHIRLWIND ROMANCE

DANNY MARTIN

I guess we never even asked for each other,
but we met and we had a laugh with each other,
went to more than a few bars with each other,
had a wiggle and a dance with each other,
laid down and looked up at the stars with each other,
grew feelings in our hearts for each other,
couldn't bear to be apart from each other,
we reached a point we would even take scars for each other,
blast for each other,
walk on broken glass for each other,
snow patrol: chasing cars for each other,
we would never ask for another.
so how have we reached a point now where we can't be asked
for each other,
is it worth asking each other?
we probably would pass on each other,
probably walk past one another,
are we living in the past of each other?
has our time passed with each other?
broken hearts for each other.
I guess we reached a point where we take scars from each
other.
We'll take with us broken shards of each other.
I guess we never even asked for each other.

PINK SKY IMITATOR
RAHEELA SULEMAN

ever since I started imitating pink skies
the local stray follows me home.
talks to me in riddles in between popping bubble-gum,
tilts its head and beckons me with its right paw.
it asks me how long it is until sunrise
and where the sun hides for the meantime.
says I remind them of a friend from a past life
but I don't make friends easily,
don't think they want to be seen with me,
I'm low in vitamin d and suicidal seasonally.
cat tells me the trees around here retired as oxygen tanks,
now they grow inside for a change of scenery.

ever since I started imitating pink skies
I set sail upon Code Lyoko
I drift above rose-tinted seas,
the seagulls fly backwards into me,
the horizon follows me for an infinity
where I'm going, I don't know.

accidental like PowerPuff.
parallel self with questionable mental health.
I am a place to call purple.
the view outside your window.
the hand on glass emulating starfish.
I am corrupted file on encrypted hard drive,
3d read like 2d,
the brick wall I shadow box with

my knuckles red when they glide
extended sigh.
I am Bart on his skateboard trying to get by,
I am sap trapped in vein under brown skin in disguise,
I droop like daisies,
I straighten out the stem like spine.

I can't spend the next 8 lives figuring out if the stray and I died
or were reborn each time.
I try to jump the synapse
I barely make it to the other side.

this mourning I left the house in black,
next week I'll laugh in yellow til I'm blue.
cat says I might turn green in between the two,
or I'll stay mimicking pink
where people look up to while they pray.
I look down as much as up,
sometimes sideways,
Insha'Allah if it's the right way.
in the wake of the earth and the wrath of the end
I just want to hug my friends.
pitch bend my voice like I do with spoons,
compare my craters with the moon,
I'm made by the same creator too.

ever since I started imitating pink skies
the cat tells me what it's like on the other side.

I learned the graveyards not the way,
but I used to fuckin try.

'CARE FOR ME' ON THE BUS RIDE HOME

PRERANA KUMAR

Caught in the corner of the window seat, I curl against your
warmth, ask why victories here still sting like the first one

when I left her, one foot snagged in a circle
of daisy-chain mines

when I turned to look back before I crossed the seas, I could
no longer tell her face
apart from the gravestones

where she smiled faintly in the showering sun, palms
outstretched as if in dance

I want to tell you how I have had torn feet since how her
voice is a tightening noose and how I still call her three times
a day to slip it around myself

I ask you for music to make me forget.
You serenade me with Care for Me and I want to tell you that
you have hands that look like they have curled God in their
palms and let go

I want to tell you to use my body like brown oilcloth to sever
your seas so you can return I give you the weight of a country
because I see the hole of one in you

I want to tell you there are daisy-chain holes
punched in me too

We leave our love in moving boxes taped shut. We carry the
grief in our backpacks and sit, shoulder-to-shoulder cadavers
full of precious, twisted heirlooms our families stacked
within us before the fire that ripped lullaby
that wilted daisy chain

Were we to Overwinter alone
I wonder how many snowflakes
they'd pick out of our death-stained teeth

But we hold red palms in a White desert and now that we've
survived across the seas, I wonder how many times they run
our red lights
without thinking

JUNGLE
LUKE AG

Most people's role models are their fathers and uncles
but he aspired to lions because he was raised in the jungle
A place filled with serpents and rubble
where you either gave up or gave praise to the struggle
But like most big cats he was trapped like it was fun
Put inside a cage where all he could do was rap to the young
Talked about the trap and the sound of the poacher's gun
The words he spat were violent, but in the lion's head, he sung.
Too much time spent within one's own mind
Makes you think you're in prison for life for only doing one
crime
Made him feel like the lion king, cos he relied too much on his
own pride
He never really recovered from when Mufasa died.
Instead he thought all of those scars were on his side
Grew up in a pack comprised mainly of sisters and mothers
So he learned his lessons listening mainly to lionesses and
brothers
They taught him that the pressure keeps on pressing, keeps
you guessing until you go
under
Unless you push down and pop up, become a star like they
wonder...

WATERFIELD ROAD

HEIDI HENDERS

The first climate refugees moved quietly,
Widely reported to be a myth.
Stiff bodied and gaunt faced,
Displaced.
Wastelands start appearing,
Searing sun and water none.
From the desert first, climate refugees move quietly.
Friday: the plants start dying on Waterfield Road.
Old trees are quivering with the soaring heat,
Beat.
Seated in a garden Mrs Jones clutches her stick,
Sick of hearing bad news and disaster tales,
Frail and stuck in her ways,
Dazed.
Blazes start on the Yorkshire Moors,
Stores empty.
Lengthy journeys from distant parts, climate refugees move
quietly.
Blindly tottering about her life, Mrs Jones doesn't notice at
first.
Worse winters and blazing springs
Brings little stress to a woman her age.
Disengaged with the daily papers,
Neighbours never home,
Alone.
Mrs Jones gardens lots, grass and hedges cut,
But then the plants start dying on Waterfield Road.
Cold winters freeze the leaves,

Bees start to disappear,
Fear.
Clean signs of a world undone,
One by one, people start leaving Waterfield Road.
Bold claims from colder nations lead to mass migration
patterns,
Fashions new grooves in ancient stones,
Thrown into disarray,
Dismay.
Away from their homes the climate refugees move louder.
Floundering in the summer haze,
Days without seeing a soul,
Mrs Jones remains inside.
Wide-eyed she's watched the road disperse.
First the families, then slowly them all,
Wall to wall traffic across the town,
Down to the coast and beyond.
Fond of this street Mrs Jones will not leave,
Breathing in the toxic air,
Unfair.

A POEM FIT FOR THE PAGE
COURTNEY AMA STODDART

When is a poem fit for a page?
Do I grab you reader?
Will you play student and I'll play teacher just for a moment?
Do my words carry your eyes across the page?
Like mother carries foetus
The words should not deplete us
These words can, repeated
Deep seated, thoughts completed
Sinking deep into subconscious and made conscious when
repeated
Can you feel my rage emanating from the black printed ink?
Do these words sink into your soul?
Can you tell that I am woman and severed black and white
not quite whole?
Will this sound like another lustful ballad of oppression?
No signs of navigation and only dim misdirection
Can you question your position in this system?
Can tears transcend paper and page to purge the Earth for
what it's worth from whence it came
To the precipice where heart and soul intertwine?
Can paper and ink create concave in the black white divide?
Can two sides coincide and bring two ends to meet on the
inside?
Would red ink be the contractual agreement in blood?
And if so, would my blood ever be enough?
Spilled across the page?
My heart, my lungs
My fingers, my thumbs

Can your ears hold the sound of my heart and my fears?
Am I psychic not seer?
Prophecies and theories dissected like surgeon and patient
And I am the patient; I'm patiently waiting without a room
We cry out for shelter and return like death to the tomb

NEW ORDER
ESTHER KOCH

Let's play a game of ocean-chess.
I could be your guppy-queen
and you could be my briny-king,
we could live in
drowned mausoleums
and with sunken sphynx
I'm talking
conical turrets and gilded cornucopia,
coral orchards, an opalescent utopia,
cowry shells, you know the ones
with baby-tooth
sing us sonnets and burble sooth,
spa-days in the Pacific Ring
and Super-Algae-health-drinks,
this is the new order of things.
The Moon is a madame
and the Sea is her whore,
the Waves are loose
and their brothel is the Shore,
the Ocean is unsentimental,
sub-zero-cruel and
anti-hero,
lauded for her treasure
the pleasure is there to simply take,
she comes in tsunami-surges
she is unbinding
suppressed urges,
she is like living in a snow globe in perpetual-shake.

We could be 30,000 feet under her
with the deep-skulking freaks,
the cerulean mystique
and the lunar light.
We could be like the Greeks
tripping between islands,
the Swordfish would cut us some gills
and the Seagoats would settle our wills on land.
We could elope with the Silence.
The Whales are cardinals of the salt,
they could sanctify our oaths to the Shoal
if our oaths mean anything, anymore...
We're punting on the planet like it's a derby,
a cold war between Earth and Water
and while I do like to be beside the Seaside
the Saline is coming up for the slaughter,
this will be the new world order
re-writing gospels in squid-ink.
Commandments on crisp sheets of seaweed,
Molluscs and Men
singing them
in the Wash,
but I fear that the end of the world as we know it will be
nothing so romantic
nothing like a manga comic
nothing like Atlantis,
the new ordinary is
polyamorous. Sleeping together

on a communal mattress, a shared bed
no longer garrotted by the nets of trawler-men
or pierced with rigs, we will be
pillowed by the Sand-drifts, where Oyster Mothers
might sing their Pearls to sleep
in the Old-Earth language.

GODS ON EARTH
SAF-S2E

Scramble for gods and earths
Precious rubble from pressured soul
Sticks and stones bodies under stone and home is unknown

All to teach of God's worth

False prophets for profit
And place faith on monetary gain

The prettiest smiles come from permanent pain
Some scars have healed but they'll all hurt the same
It rains on the sunniest days,

and they lay to sleep in the deadliest ways
There can never be enough hearse space

And every ism mirrors the last
And every year there's a new kid in class
Set apart
Named by his church
The God that burned his church
And commanded a dirty face in prayer

Blooded are the hands in the archives of history's victor
And limited are the words of a picture
Tell me what's the use of omitted scripture buried in empty
bottles of liquor?
Smoke and cherry wine to clear the mind

There's dreaded wisdom in a Guinness drunk genius.
Find me a break less system and tell me where human nature
couldn't break it,

False prophets scramble profit from gods and earths
Pickle the tabernacle flesh of the miss-sold soul
That never had a body in tomb to shift a stone door

Stuck home with Stockholm syndrome was a worshiper's
discourse
And blind faith to a black hearted light-handed father is
issues for the pretty daughter
And her faultless heart is rendered frozen by stray ice
bullets.

Forgotten are the deceived martyrs that paid high prices for
misplaced honour
Judge them not but admire their character.
He who defies first dies the worst,
He who learns first knows the truth hurts
And it hurts to know that you know nothing at all
And all you've been taught is a perspective lie.
Everything is a chase for money
Love and survival the only
counteracts to the suit
The greatest motivators of rule
The scramble for gods and earths
Behind the false prophets for profit.

And the only true lesson is that there's beauty behind the madness.

MY MOTHER'S ANTHEM IN A FOREIGN PLACE
AMINA ATIQ

Girls like us go to war every day,
we placed on our armours, tucked
in our school shirts, lifted our skirts
chasing those white boys down
double decker buses.
You racist prick, I shouted, running
down Queens Drive as he chased me
with a knife. We are forced to learn English
quicker, to save us from a stab wound in our backs.
We wore expensive running shoes, hanging
our keys around our necks,
to let them know we are coming.
Girls like us, settled in a foreign place,
we buried our mother's tongue in our back
gardens, to find the roots outgrown even deeper.
A sacrifice that haunts you every time you sing
your mother's anthem. But you keep on dancing,
around the woman in the shop who looks
at you in disgust.
Girls like us grew balls with pink bows,
we passed borders with our home
on our backs, dancing two, two step Baladi,
around the immigration officer, fluttering
my tongue, I recited my tribal name
explaining why I don't look like a Mary Jane
and I smell like my gran-ma's spices and lime.
Girls like us, are told to throw our veils
in the river, no letterbox delivers here.

You wait for Trump to blow
his Trumpet and kiss the face
of Boris Johnson,
You wait for the right wing to chant down
your street, you hide behind the curtain sucking
on your mother's olives.
But you keep on dancing, dancing
around the guy who huffs and puffs down
your neck. He mutters his hate. You
tighten your scarf and sit up to let him
know you are unpacking your bags
and settling here.
Today you are pushed by the bus driver.
Tomorrow, you are skipped in the line
by the teacher, told to speak louder
and clear, mimicked our broken English displaced
in the classroom, she tells you to seek asylum
the joke of today's lesson was me,
tomorrow is a girl like me.
Girls like us, learned how to defend ourselves.
Because some girls duck snowballs across the
road, but girls like us learned to throw rocks at their
glass windows.
He points at me how is she a scouser
because scousers are white and you're a paki.
Girls like us be-friend our enemies
because going home, is every tear behind
school bus stops, telling your mother

that today was okay, running
up the stairs before she could
see the scars on your face.
Going home, only meant singing
your mother's anthem in a foreign
place, but it's too broken to sit on your tongue
you stutter her vowels, elif, ba, ta, wahti, wahti, umti, umti.

HOW TO MAKE A BRICK
TOM DENBIGH

It is thought by many that contrary to popular legend, no
bricks were thrown at stonewall riots; handbags, shot glasses,
punches, but no bricks.

did you know
that Musical Legend and One True ally Taylor Swift
actually threw the first brick at stonewall
I was there
I saw it

though now that I think about it
it might actually have been Eddie Redmayne
who was drinking this huge Pina Colada
which was very well deserved, cos he'd just finished his
leading role in The Danish Girl where he pretended to be a
trans woman,
which was so brave
as he only got an Oscar, Bafta and Golden Globe nomination
for it.
And as he was finishing his cocktail, I remember him just
lifting up this breeze block
and yelling 'queer eye is the best thing on television'
and kicking off those riots

or wait
silly me
it might have been
huge gay icon

star of stage and screen
ballroom dancer and like truly one of the world's biggest advocates
for scientific advancement right now Ann Widdecombe,
who was actually there helping David Cameron officiate a lesbian marriage
cos Dave just adores gay weddings.
It was so beautiful
and actually In Unison that they threw that
first
all important
Stonewall Brick

that brick
that started something
a movement

movements
are made from speech mainly,
raw fresh words
born in deep soil
pulled from the ground
sticky with clay

movements are made from talk mostly,
back room chat
hugs
love really,

made from community sometimes
shared pain
shared grief
shared sugar from next door

and movements are made from voices really,
hushed ones for the woman whose wife
came back from the shop with three less teeth,
or sympathetic ones for Robert who's partner just passed and
he's got what, 4 months left now?
Look how thin he is.
or warm ones for Gary who used to give everyone
that holy, end of night, free cigarette
but lost his job
cos someone complained about the limp-wristed fairy waiter
god, a gay waiter imagine

make a brick

claw from the earth with your fingers
wet clay
or grasp people
warm as clay
and from the same soil
and beat them
till they have no air left in them

make a fire

build it high with the dry, sparrow-bones
of people
left to die
left to shrivel into whispers
into warnings

pack that pyre round
with that cold, dense anger
squatting toad like
at the bottom of your gut

light this
oven
with the pure talent
the sheer, raw creativity
of the gifts of bumboy
arse bandit
dyke
carpet munching
tranny faggot
bitch

watch flames spit into life,
feed them
with those hot
blood sprayed punches;
with the careful, sterilising of the cutlery you just ate with;
and with the sneer that that cute old lady on the bus saves up

all week;
just for you
take though
take the good
take all the good that is left I
n those wet clay
air-less people
and
bake them
not so hot they explode
but just below
at the edge of burning

sear them
into something to be thrown
something with weight.

take that
take a young thing
a growing movement
bake it into something
something with the shape of
a brick maybe
or
the shape of
a crowd
all hard edges and red
the shape of

a crowd dragged outside at 1am
on a late June night
in '69
and kicked
just one too many times

take that hard
singed lump straight from the oven

listen to it cooling for a minute

and then take this brick that probably didn't happen
was never thrown
and
make it into
power
bake it into minds
turn it into something
that never was
but is still
True
anyway

make a brick
throw it
or maybe

build with it

and then
before the fire dies
make
another

never mind
if some bricks are imaginary
just as long as you
do something real with them

The poet Allen Ginsburg remembers coming down to the
third day of the stonewall riots.
'You know, the guys there were so beautiful,' he said.
'They've lost that wounded look.'

SET HIM FREE (PART 1)
BIRDSPEED

Have you ever heard a grown man shuffle to the sounds of
his demons?
Seen his eyes blink like the wings of a butterfly?
Every time they open you witness the patterns of his
undoing.
Brown spots and familiarity.
It is easier to hear water trickle down his face
than to hear drops settle in his eyelashes
Squelching, barefoot in the same place,
the shuffle.
He listens intently to snapping locks,
twitches his limbs against the ticks.
At the crack of the signal
maybe gun
maybe war cry
maybe whistle
maybe drum
he will be ready...
Set him free,
let him saw those chains in silence.
When you hear him run,
I know, you too, will move

GIRL TAKES OFF ARMOUR AND IS SAFE
CHRISTY KU

Girl puts the sword out of arm's reach,
stores the shield under the bed with her winter clothes.
Girl's bags are unpacked, no longer hidden by the door.
Girl no longer looks for exits in rooms.
Girl is neither in flight or fight.
Girl's palms grow soft, learns to touch gently.
Girl holds hands, not wars.
Girl watches the sun set and doesn't look for wolves.
Girl no longer thinks acts of kindness are chess moves.
Girl dances, badly. Laughs anyway.
Girl has always been strong. Finally feels safe.

POSTCARD
DANNY MARTIN

We hadn't uttered his name in years. Mum's dignity choked
us every time we tried. Tongue tied, his name vanished from
our vocabulary like he that summers day.

A letterbox still stamped with his size 14 times new roman
'No junk mail' sticker shuddered.
On the welcome home mat lay a postcard of a pebbled beach.
Pictured dis-interested donkeys,
hooves treading pebbles, choreographed cheesy grinned
children straddled on their backs and a
Backdrop of a distinct Eiffel tower doused in Blackpool. No
FAO but a message only mother could
read as her eyes told us it was from him.

The armchair in which his knees bobbed our bodies until the
cushion curated curves around his Irish
legs became unwrinkled. Carefully ironed clothes could sit
where we would never dare. Christmas
turkey cut by a woman who always claimed it was a man's
job. A plate that remained cupboarded
collecting a woman's best years. A childhood where his
impression lay solar eclipse shadows over
woodchip wallpaper. An armchair left un-sat but still
carrying the weight of a woman's heart. A
postcard that stayed silent pain in a jewellery box.

He added me on Facebook last week. Profile picture of him
and the woman he left mother for

Grandchildren – choreographed cheesy grins straddled on
disinterested donkeys. Hooves treading on
a pebbled beach. Eiffel tower doused in Blackpool.

A postcard addressed to me.

THAT'S WHAT HAPPENS WHEN YOU MAKE FRIENDS UNDERWATER

RAHEELA SULEMAN

1. pink panther learns how to talk.
parakeet mimics the voice in your head.

2. you meet someone in what feels like a dream.
they say you have met before
but that can't be true because
you never fell asleep.

3. your friends were imaginary,
you'd stare at walls in case they talked.

4. a giant squid cracked the turtles shell
and the turtle still welcomed you into its home.

5. mum said you were born in a hospital.
you don't believe this,
you remember leaving the fish's mouth in a bubble.

6. at the surface the sun will greet you with a sweet kiss,
you will turn brown with affection.

7. you will rinse the blues with the blues.

8. conversation cannot suffice these waves,
you silently drift between the ones gargling while they speak.

9. you lost a few friends to the wrath of water
so now they can swim.

10. you heard Kelis playing in the sandy streets.

11. a dolphin said you spend too much time focusing on breathing.

12. you have to wear an oxygen bowl on your head when you make visits
but that's what happens when you make friends under water.

13. you found the ruins of a slimy sunken city
that looked like the one you came from.
the houses had eyes and mouths for doors,
cars and boats stacked on top of each other,
you figure that sunken vehicles come with sunken people.

14. you kick your feet in the opposite direction.

A NOTE ON CATALOGUING

PRERANA KUMAR

When they laugh
about how you are a messy heap
of twisted coat hangers and undone laundry,
you smile
You have spent your life cataloguing
Rage (red) and Love (blue)
and these things don't matter
These things don't matter when you're seven and
you hear your father on the steps
when you're ten and your mother's cheeks are stained blue
she blushes royal, your father says
his hands are red instead
when you can't tell colour from emotion
If love is blue bruises, my mother lived in holy skin
If love is blue I counted the times
he dressed me in blue overalls and say proudly
my father loved me
If love is blue,
I chipped at myself to resemble
your cerulean ceramic vase,
drooped like the necks of bluebells
you picked every morning
If love is blue,
when clock strikes midnight hues
Fed myself blueberries till I was stained sick,
crying into a bottle of pills
finding love once in a blue moon

If love is blue,
I wrote letters in blue ink all my life
If they laugh at you
for how you never stop running, say
you're making up for all the years
you stood stock still
If they laugh at you
For the papers strewn on the floor, say
you deciphered coloured footsteps instead, say
It's easier to file papers in sets
Than to fish out blue bruises from your skin
All those years you thought rage and love
were the same and waited
for the footsteps to get closer
All those years you only loved the sky
when it was black night,
searched for blue roses and didn't fucking realise why
they weren't as common as the red ones
didn't fucking realise why love isn't blue
but rage is.
Until one day they said there's a reason we blush red
Until one day, you did.
You see, you did organise many, many
Difficult things in your own way
and you were really bloody good at it
You cannot explain any of this without feeling
the blue shadows that stayed all these years

So you smile and end with
If love is blue, I wouldn't have written this poem
at twenty,
I would have catalogued
Right at five

POLITICS OF THE PANSIES

LUKE AG

I've been thinking back about places I've visited
and I've got this one estate in mind
It's the first time I realised that hood mentality
is just an estate of mind
Nobody there really cares about the daily grind
as long as their smoking on their daily grind
Dandelions grow in the gardens
where there could've been roses
You could've heard the birds
if it weren't for the mopeds
Could've had progress,
if it wasn't for the posers
But that's the difference between
Dandelions and Roses
It's a bit like people...
For a rose to grow, it needs care and love
but Dandelions grow up around
a load of thugs
They grow up through the pavements
in our inner cities
When I was younger, I used to look down
and think they were pretty
But as I got older, I started to look down on them
with pity
In class we were taught that,
Dandelions are weeds
So they don't do so well in the school
Their aesthetic appearance is the only reason

we consider them fools
But they hear this too
So they stop following the rules
You always hear them say
'if they don't respect me
then why should I respect them
Just because I look different
doesn't mean I'm not as good
as any of those rose-tinted mandem
I still got value
and I still got flowers
so why don't you allow this?
Cos not looking at the bigger picture
is just plain cowardice
if you smoothed out the pavements
and funded urban developments
then I'd look just like the roses
and you'd feel far less benevolent'
The Roses look down on the Dandelions
they call them silly
They haven't got worry about this
when they're hanging out with the Lilies
But it's not their fault either
they too grew up with disparity
and just because they're young, doesn't mean that
they don't understand classism
as an everyday reality
They grew up in the suburbs

and the gardens
And most of them are just younger clippings
of their mothers and fathers
They grow up right next to them in their
picket fence paradise
with people looking down, admiring them
most of their life.
But, back on the estate the government
gives the Dandelions drugs and pesticides
Believing that's where societal
problems reside
The Dandelions rarely open their eyes
they just sniff up the nutrients from
the pills and lines
Dandelions have to grow up quickly
and it's not because they're driven
They're just dealing with the harsh situation
which they've been given
Many of them have to grow up alone
and it's really hard to see from where their
seeds are sown
Which is kind of the same as kids
who grow up in broken homes
Though, they're the same as the Roses
just looking for the light
But born too close to the road
If they were born too close to the picket fences
They're more likely to be picked

Too close to the road
They're more likely to get nicked
Doesn't matter where they are though,
They're all more likely to be kicked
So most of them look pretty battered
By age twenty-six
You don't have to be a professional botanist
to understand the problems with our pseudo-populous
Maybe even our politicians get off on this
looking down at the people with the
wrong end of the binoculars
The issue is
The beauty of the flower
Is how we determine worth
but we never stop to think about
the quality of the earth

SLEEPY JEAN
HEIDI HENDERS

It's the 23:40 service.
The train is filled with the smell of a late-night chip shop stop
People are smiling, wiling the time away with drunken jokes
and stargazing in train tunnels
I catch the eye of a tired looking guy, he looks like another
victim of the nine to fives
But on Friday night he's kicked back, stayed out a little later, a
break in the corporate escalator
And the buzz and hum of life over my headphones has me
faltering in my thoughts that everything is
going wrong
Because clearly on this last train life goes on
It's the 23:40 service
But I can't help but feel that outside this rose-tinted carriage
the stops we're headed for are dark
The train begins to slow
An old woman hauls herself up, doddering with stick in hand,
She looks back
'Where's Jack?'
Her daughter has tact, to guide her to the platform,
Like this outburst is the norm
And I wonder how long this will last
Long enough for the tax on the loss of her mind to do the
rounds?
Or will the winter winds grind her down while she sits in her
dressing gown?
It's the 23:40 service.
The train speeds up and a sleeping child stirs

A father strokes her hair, sweeping her cares from her brow
and smiling at his pride and joy.
He has a little girl and a little boNo wait.
It's only been three months, and the cuts are still deep, the
moment haunts his sleep, his little boy
flailing and failing to breathe. And now he grieves, and he
can't believe he's gone.
And he's moving out his council house.
3 bedrooms.
A disease and a cry and I don't know why but that makes a
spare room.
And that is far too expensive.
It's the 23:40 service
And I'm tired.
From the day, from the way I try, and I try to detach from the
lies, and I despise those who go
through life with closed eyes because one day they will blink,
and see we stand on the brink of a
sinkhole of society, and there's only so much we'll ever get to
be, because this Government needs
there to be poverty. They thrive on desperation and fear, and
distract us with gossip and cheap
prices for beer, and from the corner of the carriage I hear
'CHEER UP SLEEPY JEAN!'
And I glance around and they're singing and laughing, and
dancing in the aisles
And their minds are miles from the halls of Westminster.
And it's all smiles, because despite it all

they're happy.
And as they sing, I give myself over to the daydream
believers. And then if time could freeze us, it
would seem that all was right in the world.
It's the 23:40 service.
And the train pulls into its final station
Tomorrow the trains will fill again, and the wheels will turn,
and the rich will earn.
And before long it'll be 23:40 once more
And life will go on through the carriage door.

EMANCIPATE
COURTNEY AMA STODDART

Emancipate the enslavement of humanity
Eradicate the white supremacist vanity
Colonial occupation of Africa took place so callously with
excessive force and brutality
Under false illusion of a sense of rationality
Now worldwide skin bleaching becomes banality
Governments and politicians have the audacity to declare
'greatness' based on nationality
Rewrite barbaric history as victory
As if they did not aggressively manipulate, physically and
mentally – enslave and rape
Only to create international population dependency on the
British nation
Based on missionaries, 'fair trade' and mass degradation
So where is the African holocausts reparations?
Lest we not forget Britain enslaved civilisations
That had been writing and building
With advancements previously unseen
By France, the Netherlands and the Portuguese
If your economy depends upon racialized slavery
It does not bode well for your foreign policy
If your philosophy is found to be based on nothing other
than hypocrisy
In 9000BC Africa had astronomical observatories
But European settlers were more concerned with individual
luxuries
So where is the truth and why is not told?
Because the truth is worth less than lies in gold

The truth won't allow educated people to be sold
If whites thought that black was not equated with
The apes and monkeys
It would be a lot harder to let them swing dead from trees
Or transport them on slave ships across the seas
Full of rats, death, dirt and disease,
Either dying before they reach their destination
Or to be enslaved for life upon a sugar plantation
In Brazil your average life expectancy
From the moment of you arrived till the day you no longer
survived
Was only 7 years
And that's because you were worked to death let's make that
very clear
And back in Africa invaders played on existing differences
Tried to rearrange what truth and wisdom is
Tell one group that they're better
Tell one group that they're worse
This parallel throughout history has become quite the curse,
If history was a song
We're the chorus divided from the verse
And given no dress rehearsal in the play
We've been given a part with no words to say
So the Capitalist system
And its intrinsic white vision
Has commodified the black form
And they've made being white like it's just the norm
That's why so many young white people think that being

black is cool'
But they wouldn't think that if they had been racially abused
in school
Not just by pupils
But by the whole system too
Felt dirty all your life
Feel so in fear from the world
You're defensive without thinking twice
Cause you're growing up as someone who isn't white.
They listen to rap and they listen to grime,
But do they understand
The socio-economic reasons why people commit crime
It's like Listening to Bob Marley
Without exploring Marcus Garvey
Hailing the former as just a performer,
A cheeky Rasta who just wanted to get high
Ignored is the political message he had before he died
Marley is unequivocally black power
Just like Lauryn Hill he recognised the final hour,
Sought to empower generations of black and mixed-race kids
Cause he knew exactly what white privilege is

TUTANKHAMUNS

ESTHER KOCH

Don't show anyone humility.
Do not bathe another person's feet.
We are already cleansed
in the salt we secrete,
as you trudge through the city
be the city,
there's nothing straightforward about life
is curbed is potholed is one-way streets
is embossed
with braille for the blind and banisters for the weak
soft gradients for the uneasy of feet
double yellow and spikes for the cheats
You are not a cheat.
Even climbers on Kilimanjaro overreach
police officers err and falter on the beat and
babes hesitate at the teat,
everyone takes shortcuts
everyone gets lost
in payday loans and healthcare costs
and every night the sky depletes...
there are stars that have shone for light-years
that still remain to be seen
they've lost faith in our eyes and
so they abort
baby protostars and haggard red dwarfs
old boys new boys
from every walk of life.
Turn out their light.

And in Manchester
underground steam flues provide
saunas in the street
grub-on-the-grid
meals on the lattice and
dinner al-Tesco
when there is nowhere warmer to eat.
Sudden gridlock between the eaves
during the hustling hours
where each gives
what the other needs
humanity, pleated like a concertina
burgeons and recedes
at once a dirge on repeat
and a tempo
that will move you to your feet.
We need to revolutionise
our slight of tongue.
Beggars do believe.
Beggars can choose.
Those weary carves deserve DeepHeat
if only the heart could be massaged
like the back of our hung
necks would yield like a swan's
as it yearns for bread
life would rush back in through our cavities
and it feels like a menthol sweet, a hot bath, Tiger Balm and
aniseed

with only your own story
to whisper you to sleep.
2000 gods seem better than one
but by dawn they're all gone
no heifer-headed mother to usher on your heartbeat
but every new day is a papyrus sheet
in the tome of your life
that you will
we must
complete
the people will publish it.
Whether it's chipped into cinnamon stone in Petra
scribbled in playground chalk
inscribed in wet cement
or in blood
on Downing Street doors
sewn into tapestries
chanted in monasteries
encrypted onto the dark-net
stamped on the pills we take
your story in grit
around the Queen's
head on every coin we make
every penny you've handled
has passed through my hands first.
It's drunk
it's gambled
it's popped from foil bluster packs

dropped and trampled
back pocketed for good fortune
it's my quetiapine
it's her quinoa
it's your-Morrison's meal-deal
and it's his methadone,
every back alley
is a Valley of the Kings
but wealth is not genetic
and it shouldn't be an heirloom
majesty is not measured in things but I might just leave a
name in hieroglyphs, a packed lunch and some cigarettes so that
dying young and alone and unknown
it might just feel like home on the other side
of this city
there are too many
Tutankhamuns.

CLEAN HANDS
SAF-S2E

The colours are burned, and the lyrics are dead
the trees are bare
and the summer is scarce
the bars are rare
and the covers are blank
remedy remedy remedy
to mother we seek
some sages to burn
some bushes to breathe
the barren land where the blood moon screams
the ocean is green, and the mountains are warm
the sky is black the sun is out
see your memory they gave you to themselves
we stand, and clean hands

we stand,
to seek a remedy of fallen sin
to seek the memory of reformed jin
to kiss the millipede of lifetimes will
we stand to seek a rose gold fog

Hollow belly blank chest
smoke eccentric old self
stole me to new home, now how do I find sleep

The solemn hope of falsified home
the swollen intuition of foreign blood palm
oil of orangutan tears

a pale awakening of self-preservation
executed in swift motion in potion of
power possession
peep the blindest

They see what we wish to feel.
True blindness has functioning eyes.

See your memory and hope to feed your
children's children's children some food for thought

bear in mind their history is miss homed
and they will charge for their attendance at the reunion

we stand, to clean our hands

we stand, we stand
to seek a remedy of fallen sin
to seek the memory of reformed jin
to kiss the millipede of lifetimes will
we stand to seek a rose gold fog

Belly of the beast hope it shits them
Fuck the energy of enemy's backhanded apology
no question
one option
spray a choppa to bleed the bidders at the auction

Loaning artefacts that's henna tatting to cover history scars

Loaning stolen artefacts that's a temporary cover of history scars

So deep the dying star at society's cradle
the red sun is a fading fable
overfill the Nile with Human X's blood
shed in the name of shame and lust
the welcome came first, and the suffering still lasts
so plead to the benevolence that took a life
the daunted angel that sacrificed
a friend to the trail of a phoenix tail
the burning eye of desire
a day where love's for hire
the higher the mind the blacker the sacks the buller the sacks
a soul the reprogrammed a system that sold secrets to a
filtered ear
the passion of a tear
the burning of a horizontal cross
lay down the weapons of a loss
The war to end all wars will end with no survivors
so drop this soul on a never ending fall and it will feel just at
home
a permanent sleep is all we have guaranteed.
Peace, love and unity the sanctity needed by all and one
we stand, to clean our hands.

THE SUBURB OF BASRA
AMINA ATIQ

Name: Muayad Ahmad Jalaf
Occupation: A lecturer at the Arts College, Basra University.
Death: September, 12, 2017.
Hope is born again in the faces of
the streets – we are forced to forget but
we think we hear a whisper echoing in
the distance – it is death in a figure of
A group of armed young men
Three cars
A government plate
If only war was enough to endure fragmented souls and
shattered
dreams. But he didn't return home his body lay in the Basra
suburb.
Hope died again the faces of the
streets – funeral bells, chanting men
and mourning families – if only the truth
unveiled itself so justice can conquer but the blood is swept
from the streets
so they may dance again.
But the music has grown numb and his
name lingers in our history books.
Time will heal and the truth will
uncover itself in your white sheets.
In honour we remember – in justice
we tie his name on the tip of our lips and very suburb will
call his
name and we will follow.

BIRTH OF TRICKSTER

TOM DENBIGH

he used to eat the scabs on
his knees peeling them and
then between his fingers
making them into a crunchy
snail strawberry rollup kind
of a snack
scaly legs he had such scaly little
skinny legs from the kicks the other
boys gave him wore them like it was
deliberate legs half ringed round
looking like bird claws and rat tails
little shifty skinny nerd boy of uncertain
parentage books held to chest with half
a dozen elbows flapping round like
pushed out, cuckoo-ed chick
scaly legs look
at scaly legs
little scabby
legs rich with
old cuts
peeling flap
flap raven boy
little giant
fox-like
smile
twitching
ears scaled
whip of a

thing, lilting
spider-boy
so many
names none
of them
right prince
of lies
he started growing into
 a seesaw of a man
changeling thing no
 wonder they kicked him
really not on our
doorstep please
until they found needles in all their
sandwiches one screaming bite too
late, but he was so kind to the younger
children with his offerings strawberry
laces flowing out of paper bags,
sewing mouths shut with one
hand feeding the hungry
with another
there were many of him in
school my town had three
skinny little nasty scale-legged
boys
creepy things tricking
leopards out of their
spots bringing fire and

misery left right and
centre good for colour
but not here thank you
kick them some more till
you see them flying
away from town with big
black wings better hope
they don't come back
scab eating raven boys
sowing what you reap

SET HIM FREE (PART 2)
BIRDSPEED

Bodies stretched towards the stars and left to rot on wood,
or to become it. Arrived like wet mahogany, soiled and above
the ground. Hearts disordered and hung. The boy stumbles
in his blocks. Presses down into the Earth before attempting
to spring like a cricket into air. While the clay floor sleeps,
he pounds his feet to imitate thunder in the sky, they harden
like fresh yam. On the gun or whistle he will attempt to tear
into the night, to find lightening. If he does, he will become a
demi-God and live among us. Set him free, let him run, so we
can protect our dreams.

Photo: Bethany Baker

Christy Ku

Christy Ku is a Hong Kong born up-and-coming London based creative. She has performed across the country at venues including Hoxton Hall, The Pit Theatre, Broadway Barking and at the Walthamstow Garden Party. Christy has also worked closely with the Barbican Centre as a Barbican Young Poet and as a creator and performer for the show *A Change is Gonna Come* in collaboration with Boy Blue Entertainment.

Christy is also short story writer, YouTube journalist, digital content producer, photographer and creator of the podcast *A Long Way Out.*

She is currently working towards her debut poetry collection and various other projects.

Danny Martin

Danny Martin is a north-west London born performer and storyteller. His aim is to tell and capture true stories through poetry, his own and that of people from his communities. Danny endeavours to story tell vividly to build characters, places and moments of time.

He describes himself as 'A Gogglebox of poetry'. In performance, Danny highlights an inspiration for his poetic style as the streets, the hard-hitting lyricism and casual delivery speaks volumes for his work.

Raheela Suleman

Raheela means 'happy journey'. She is a former Barbican Young Poet and a member of Octavia Poetry Collective. Her most recent film was made in collaboration with Channel 4, the ICA and Chisenhale Gallery and she is a Film Studies graduate. She also makes beats in her bedroom under the name 'eyeglitch' and paints.

She was born in London but is open to being buried elsewhere.

Prerana Kumar

Prerana Kumar is an Indian spoken word artist whose poetry revolves around love, loss and identity. She is a member of the Writer's Squad (2018-2020). She is the winner of the Say Owt Slam 2018 and also a member of the Durham Slam Team who came 3rd at UniSlam 2019, where she also won Verve's Poet of the Slam prize for best individual performance.

Luke AG

Luke AG is a London based poet with a distinctly political and historical message. He uses poetry and rhyme to navigate through a narrative of his own life, and the people around him. Originally from Hastings, a lot of his poems work through his journey from a small town to the big city, with a couple of pit stops along the way.

Heidi Henders

Heidi is a poet and theatre-maker based in the north-west of England. Having completed a degree in Contemporary Theatre and Performance she now endeavours to create in theatre and poetry, implementing content that can inspire and encourage social change, exploring the world we live in.

SAF-S2E

Safwat Elsenossi, known as SAF-S2E, is a poet and rapper. He began writing at the age of 14 and first performed at BBC Radio 1Xtra Words First 2015. He is a member part of Manchester's Young Identity and has been in productions such as Breathe and Breathe 2 produced by New York's The Dream Ring, Manchester International Festival (MIF) and Young Identity.

Courtney Ama Stoddart

Courtney Stoddart is a poet and singer passionate about dismantling hierarchy in all its forms. She intertwined elements of historical, political and social discussion into rhythm and rhyme. Taking inspiration from the lyricism and format of old school hip hop and rap.

He was also featured on BBC Radio 5 Afternoon edition along with four other Young Identity poets as well as performing at the British Council Literature Seminar held in Berlin in January 2019. He has also performed at Sounds From The Other City Festival 2018 & 2019, Moovin Festival 2018, Dot to Dot Festival 2019 and Latitude Festival 2019.

Amina Atiq

Amina Atiq is a Yemeni-Scouse writer, performance artist, workshop facilitator and activist.

She has been featured on various artistic platforms such as BBC Radio 5 live, BBC Radio 6 music, The Independent, British Muslim TV @thewarehouse, Writing on the Wall, Skinny magazine, Whispering Dialogue, CAAT, Human Appeal and many more.

Her recent work involves co-writing a play with Ice Fire Theatre, which was premiered in the Liverpool Arab Arts Festival 2018. In collaboration with LAFF, she has partnered with Liverpool and Leeds University in delivering its first ever national arts engagement project-funded by the British Academy.

Amina was awarded the LJMU Citizenship award for her active and community engagement work and awarded the best North West volunteer by Human Appeal. She was long listed for the Jerwood Poetry Fellowship and awarded as a Young Associate for Curious Minds.

Tom Denbigh

Tom is a Bristol based poet and producer. His wickedly beautiful writing holds up a distorted mirror to the world. Deftly weaving the queer experience alongside tales of friends and strangers, he toys with myth, devilish humour, and absurdity to portray the bizarre and brilliant in the everyday.

Birdspeed

British born Barbadian raised artist, Birdspeed is the 2019 UK Hammer & Tongue National Poetry Slam Champion. Her work has been captivating audiences across the UK and the US. She has also facilitated workshops in a variety of organisations including a men's prison. Her work can also be found in the *Words on Windrush Anthology* (Empowered, July 2019) and *The Alter Egos Anthology* (Bad Betty Press, 2019). Birdspeed's debut pamphlet *Bloom* (2019) is available on her website

Esther Koch

Esther Koch has been writing and performing spoken word, page poetry and prose for 6 years. She is a slam winning stage poet and as a member of the Mancunian collective Young Identity she has showcased her work at BBC Radio 1xtra's Words First, HOME, UniSlam, alongside the BBC Philharmonic Orchestra at the Sounds From The Other City festival and the collective's own One Mic Stand. She has also supported celebrated poets such as Benjamin Zephaniah and Saul Williams. Esther is a dedicated presence on the Manchester and Salford open mic poetry scene and can be seen and heard at regular events such as SpeakEasy, Bad Language, That's What She Said, Verbose and Salford's late and much lorded Evidently.

Esther is motivated by the socio-political environment in which she lives, as well as the wider topics of race, religion, colour, mental and physical health and the female experience. She supports local charities and fundraising events as a performer when she can. Esther works at Salford Foodbank and is set to recommence study at Salford University this September, reading International Politics and Security.

About OWN IT!

OWN IT! is a storytelling lifestyle
brand, sharing stories across books,
music, art and film. At the heart
of everything we do is a desire to
share, empower, celebrate and
inspire. Whether it's through multi-
media digital books, print books,
music or film, OWN IT! releases
original and authentic stories told
in creative new ways.

About Wrecking Ball Press

Since 1997 Wrecking Ball Press
has published high quality, cutting
edge literature, building a national
reputation that far exceeds its size.
This is based on a commitment to
connecting the most innovative
and accessible novels and poetry
with a readership not traditionally
associated with literature.
Wrecking Ball Press has a strong
record of discovering exciting first
time writers, many of whom have
gone on to have further commercial
and critical success with larger
publishers.